The Bad Hair Day BOOK

A PICK ME UP! BOOK

COUNTRYMAN ®

A Division of Thomas Nelson Publishers

Since 1798

www.thomasnelson.com

Published by J. Countryman® a division of Thomas Nelson, Inc., Nashville, Tennessee 37214

Editorial development by Mark Gilroy Communications
Managing editor: Jessica Inman

For a list of acknowledgements, see page 220.

www.jcountryman.com
www.thomasnelson.com

Designed by Thinkpen Design, LLC, Fayetteville, Arkansas

ISBN 1404103759

Printed and bound in the United States of America

Contents

A Little Help, Please 175

Oh Yeah, Looking Good! 199

Acknowledgements 220

TANGLES

Life is inherently messy.
But out of the messiness
comes great things.

MARGARET WHEATLY

"Okay, gang, let's get moving. We're running late and I want to get there in time. Everyone to the car, now!"

Uh-oh. Where did I put the keys to the van?

Yep, life gets tangled up. Just read "I Lost My Sanity on the Road to Phoenix" and you'll know you're not alone!

But even in the midst of life's complications, it is possible to keep your act together—and maybe even smile. It would help, of course, if you could find the keys to the car.

GIVE YOUR WORRIES TO THE LORD,
AND HE WILL TAKE CARE OF YOU.

PSALM 55:22

Perfect is never doing anything wrong—which means never doing anything at all.

STEPHEN MANES

I Lost My Sanity on the Road to Phoenix

ELAINE YOUNG MCGUIRE

I failed Motherhood 101 one day when I failed to use fabric softener. I always use it—except when I run out or have no idea where it is, as was the case when unpacked moving boxes filled our new house in Phoenix.

It had been a hard move from Atlanta. I don't recommend a family driving two cars and four children cross-country even during the best of times. This wasn't.

Near the end of the process of adopting one of my students, my husband's job transfer suddenly materialized. "Don't worry," our case manager assured us, "we'll transfer custody from Georgia to Arizona, and you can take her with you as you leave town." But all the paperwork in the world couldn't make our highway journey a cakewalk.

The next two days blurred as I followed Jim's car. Our biggest excitement was watching flashing blue lights approach. "I'm not giving you a ticket, ma'am," the officer drawled. "I know you were just trying to keep up with your husband."

On weekend trial visits to our home, the tiny sixth grader had seemed as meek and passive as she was in my class. Now, cooped up in a car, loudly demanding her choice of music, I barely recognized her.

She often forgot her new status and raised her hand to speak. "Mrs.

McGuire—oops, *Mom*—I have to get a bathing suit." The next minute it was a pair of name-brand shoes that she had to get immediately. Her dreams of being adopted had included fantasies of the perfect family, which meant getting anything you wanted.

Halfway across Texas, my husband complained, "Honey, I feel awful." I felt his head—he had a raging fever.

"I feel bad too," echoed our eleven-year-old diabetic son. Testing revealed John was approaching diabetic coma.

Later that night, we cajoled a doctor into coming to the motel. "Flu," he pronounced over Jim. "Ma'am, your husband needs bed rest and lots of fluids—get to Phoenix as quickly as you can. And watch your boy closely. Be sure he gets exercise and the right foods."

The next two days blurred as I followed Jim's car. Our biggest excitement was watching flashing blue lights approach. "I'm not giving you a ticket, ma'am," the officer drawled. "I know you were just trying to keep up with your husband."

Jim winked at me and whispered, "I was just trying to get out of your way." He was right. I was the one with the lead foot.

He drove slowly after that, slumped over the wheel, hazy eyes attempting focus. At each "pit stop," he slept in the back seat until I returned with whatever "flu food" I could scrounge.

"Run around and around the car," I commanded John, "and eat every last bite of your food." Clay and Melissa, our two youngest, scrunched down in the seat, arguing who would have to ride with Dad next. It hadn't even occurred to me to wonder if I'd packed fabric softener.

We arrived in the Valley of the Sun during a fierce storm. I would have been more appreciative if I'd known we wouldn't see rain again for nearly a year.

Jim collapsed at the motel, dutifully sipping another Sprite. Martha wondered what kind of family they had given her to when I hollered,

"Let's get out of here. Daddy needs some quiet."

I drove carefully, squinting at street signs and blinded by headlights reflected in the slick streets, until I located a large mall. As we spiraled around in the parking garage, I prayed I'd quickly find a theatre. Lucky me—I found it before the movie ended.

Our second day in the motel, Jim awoke and pronounced himself cured. We drove on.

His new job had promised less travel and more family time, so it seemed like a cruel joke when he was sent out of town for days immediately after our arrival. Poor guy.

Meanwhile, the children and I unpacked and settled into our new neighborhood. I quickly located a diabetic specialist, found a grocery store, and stocked the pantry with essentials. When I attacked the mountain of dirty clothes, I realized I'd forgotten fabric softener on my shopping list.

The "something" was Martha's new training bra, firmly and cruelly pinned to her sweater by static electricity.

When Jim returned home he said, "I've looked up addresses of nearby churches. Why don't we go to a different one each service until we find one we like, one with a good youth program for the kids?"

We liked the friendly people at the churches we attended Sunday morning and Sunday night, but all four children felt intimidated going into their individual classes. We insisted, believing this would help them connect quickly with new Christian friends.

Wednesday night we were in a mad rush getting ready to attend midweek classes at a third church, which met in a school. "Where are my jeans?" Clay called.

"They're still in the washer," I hollered back.

"Where is my white sweater?" Martha asked.

"In the dryer," I replied.

We hurried to the car, found the school, but arrived a little late. The children seemed anxious, "What if they don't like us? Everyone makes fun of our accents."

Jim and I encouraged them, "Just be yourselves. You'll do fine." But at this point, the kids had experienced about all the "new" they could handle, especially Martha.

We had trouble locating everyone's classes, scattered around the large facility. Younger ones first, we reasoned. At last we found Martha's room and then, finally, our own.

After classes, we reassembled at the car. "How did it go?" we asked, smiling.

Martha burst into tears. "Oh, Mom, it was awful. I was so late I had to walk to the front of the room to find a seat."

After class, a girl had tapped her shoulder. Martha thought she was being welcomed, but then the girl whispered, "There's something on the back of your sweater."

The "something" was Martha's new training bra, firmly and cruelly pinned to her sweater by static electricity. Saying, "Oh, honey, I'm so sorry," felt so inadequate, but at least I had the sense to promise right then that she'd never have to go back there.

We survived. Now, almost thirty years later, that little blonde, blue-eyed sixth grader has become the nearly perfect parent of our five almost perfect grandchildren. They have a mother who always—and I do mean always—washes every load of laundry with the very best fabric softener on the market. ⬡

WE ALSO HAVE JOY WITH OUR TROUBLES, BECAUSE
WE KNOW THAT THESE TROUBLES PRODUCE PATIENCE.

ROMANS 5:3

Spin Cycle

If you're feeling frazzled, maybe your spirit needs a cleansing change of routine. This week, do something brand new: Borrow some rollerblades and go for a spin through the park (make sure you have a helmet and ample padding for your elbows and knees!). Sign up for a dance class. Grab a pencil and sketchpad and find a scenic spot to draw or write. Or, just sleep late. A revitalizing break from your usual regimen might be just what you need to chase away the frizzies of your hair and soul.

They Said It

The Airplane Law: When the plane you are on is late,
the plane you want to transfer to is on time.
AUTHOR UNKNOWN

Everything is funny as long as it is happening to somebody else.
WILL ROGERS

If you wonder where your child left his roller skates,
try walking around the house in the dark.
LEOPOLD FECHTNER

God grant me the serenity to accept the people I cannot change,
the courage to change the one I can, and the wisdom to know it's me.
AUTHOR UNKNOWN

The day will happen whether or not you get up.
JOHN CIARDI

So many tangles in life are ultimately hopeless that
we have no appropriate sword other than laughter.
GORDON W. ALLPORT

It is not fancy hair, gold jewelry, or fine clothes that should make you beautiful. No, your beauty should come from within you—the beauty of a gentle and quiet spirit that will never be destroyed and is very precious to God.

1 PETER 3:3-4

*Some days you
tame the tiger.
And some days the
tiger has you for lunch.*

TUG MCGRAW

Think You're Having a Bad Day?

JERRY LANE

It was Diane's turn to open the bank. On such mornings, as was protocol, she unlocked the door and entered the bank without disengaging the alarm, only punching in her code on the keypad to disarm the alarm after checking to make sure all was secure inside the bank. If the security company didn't receive a disarm signal after forty-five seconds, they notified the police.

Unfortunately, she had woken up feeling fluish and nauseated this particular day. Knowing that a) the bank opened a couple hours earlier than most, and b) if she called anyone to sub for her that early in the morning, she might lose the luxury of having air in her tires at the end of the workday, she decided she could at least open the bank and then go home to get well.

She drove up to the lot, rushed in, looked around, and didn't see anyone. Growing sicker by the moment, she hurriedly gave the all-clear signal to the tellers. Unfortunately, she forgot one little procedure—disarming the alarm.

The tellers came in and Diane bustled out the door. Meanwhile, the police had taken their place behind a building. Diane—in old jeans and an old shirt and carrying her oversized purse which evidently looked like a suitable one for robbing banks—jumped into her older-model van and sped away.

The police immediately tailed her and turned on their lights. She reluctantly pulled onto the side of the road. At the exact same moment, her son happened to pass by on the school bus, saw her getting pulled over, and called her on his cell phone. She reached into her purse to answer the phone just as the officers began to get out of their vehicle. Thinking Diane was reaching for a firearm and believing she had just robbed a bank, the policemen drew their weapons and ordered, "Drop your weapon, raise both hands, get out slowly, and step away from the vehicle."

Unfortunately, she forgot one little procedure—disarming the alarm.

Pale-faced and shaking, she dropped the phone and complied with their requests. One officer approached, gun in hand, while the other one backed him up. Diane began explaining with her hands in the air as he got closer. Beads of sweat accumulated on her forehead, which the officer took as a sure sign of lying. As he stepped right in front of her to question her further, Diane, unable to hold her sickness at bay any longer, summarily threw up all over the policeman.

Obviously, some bad days are worse than others. Sometimes you spill your coffee in the car; other times you are falsely accused of grand larceny and deface the uniform of one of the city's finest. But all bad days have one thing in common: They only last twenty-four hours. ⬡

THE LORD'S LOVE NEVER ENDS;
HIS MERCIES NEVER STOP.
THEY ARE NEW EVERY MORNING;
LORD, YOUR LOYALTY IS GREAT.

LAMENTATIONS 3:22-23

Joke Break

These jokes may be "groaners," but they might be just right for fighting off those petty annoyances of life.

Doctor, I keep forgetting things.
When did this start happening?
When did what start happening?

Doctor, my hair keeps falling out.
Can you give me something to keep it in?
How about a paper bag?

What did the porcupine say to the cactus?
Is that you, Mama?

*Life is made up, not of
great sacrifices or duties,
but of little things,
in which smiles, and
kindnesses, and small
obligations, given
habitually, are what
win and preserve the
heart and secure comfort.*

HUMPHREY DAVY

One Hug to Go, Please

NANCY B. GIBBS

The lunch crowd packed the small restaurant. As a handful of waitresses tried to serve the many diners, a family of four made rude remarks regarding the service and the father spoke harshly to his waitress. She rushed to the kitchen and picked up a tray filled with food, balancing it precariously. In her rush back to the family's table, a plate fell from her tray and shattered. After a stunned half-second, the waitress broke down and cried.

From the next table, a woman stood up without a word and gave the waitress a hug. The waitress cried on her shoulder for a few seconds before cleaning up the dish. When the waitress returned to the family's table, the father apologized to her, and a smile returned to her face.

It's funny how powerful kind actions are—they can bring out the best in people, even under the most strained and frantic of circumstances. ⬢

The great secret that all old people share is that you really haven't changed in seventy or eighty years. Your body changes, but you don't change at all. And that, of course, causes great confusion.

DORIS LESSING

A Girdle by Any Other Name

TSGOYNA TANZMAN

It's nothing new. For hundreds of years, women have sucked in their sagging flab and tried various ways of rearranging their recalcitrant tummies and thighs.

As the years passed, I witnessed my own kind of continental drift. Slowly but surely, various body parts shifted southward and my center mass took on new territories to the east and west. I discovered its full-blown effect while shopping for a dress for an afternoon wedding. "May I show you something in a sheath?" a sales assistant offered.

Show, she said. She had no idea how prophetic her word choice was. As it happened, everything showed: saddlebags, a pouchy tummy and, shall we say, a less than perky derriere.

"Don't worry," she said, "we have these wonderful body shapers in foundations."

What was she talking about? Were there fitness trainers in the cosmetics department? Then it dawned on me. "You're talking about a girdle, aren't you?"

"We like to call them body shapers in this new millennium," she countered, her voice dripping with condescension.

As I rode up the escalator to lingerie, I rehearsed how I'd ask for this alleged "body shaper." Swaggering up to the counter, I sized up the nubile twentysomethings behind the cash register.

"Girls," I began, "I'm looking for a girdle. Call it whatever you like, but I need a girdle."

Stripped bare in the dressing room, I examined myself from every angle in the three-paneled mirror, anticipating the smoothing effects of these so-called body shapers. Would my tummy be instantly transformed into a graceful hourglass? Or would stepping into a newfangled girdle be more like putting a rubber band around a pillow?

The sales girl interrupted my thoughtful moment with a knock and an armload of the newest inventions designed to lift, separate, and flatten.

"You can start with the tiniest brief and work your way up to the full body shaper if you need more slimming," she chirped, then disappeared.

Feeling hopeful, I searched for what she referred to as the tiniest brief. "You must've forgotten the 'brief,'" I hollered toward the top of the door, "because there's nothing in here that's 'small and lacking length!'"

I grabbed the smallest swath of fabric—the size of a small couch cushion—and pulled it on. As I struggled to breathe, I realized it was all a matter of physics: If you squish something here, it will pop out there. Yep, my stomach was definitely flatter, but now there was flab hanging over the top of the elastic, and I don't even want to talk about the brand-new upper thigh flab that suddenly materialized. Next.

I crammed myself into another full-legged brief. (Why were they still calling these things "briefs," anyway?) This one lifted my rear and tightened around my thighs, but now my knees bulged. Finally, I tried the full-slip shaper complete with bra, but no matter how I adjusted the straps, the effect was somehow closer to inner tube than hourglass.

"Oh, and you might want to try this," the sales girl knocked. "This one's not so tight and it looks more like bike pants." Perfect, I thought as I slipped into this latest torture device. If I'm in an accident, they'll think I'm athletic.

To my pleasant surprise, nothing bulged or hung out, and as a bonus feature, I could still breathe. I pulled on my shirt and elastic-waist pants and marched out to pay.

As I stood in line, I felt the need to share this rite of passage with someone. So I shouldered up to the woman buying a lacy D-cup bra and thong.

"You know," I said, "it's a lot more fun buying your first bra than it is your first girdle."

Fondling her miniscule thong, she turned away—as if buying a girdle might be contagious. Okay, so thong-lady didn't share my moment, but it was no less epiphanous; because, in that instant, I finally understood what older women have been talking about for years. They say that as a woman ages, she grows more comfortable in her own skin.

Trust me, they're not waxing philosophical—it's simply roomier.

EVEN WHEN YOUR HAIR HAS TURNED GRAY, I WILL TAKE CARE OF YOU. I MADE YOU AND WILL TAKE CARE OF YOU. I WILL CARRY YOU AND SAVE YOU.

ISAIAH 46:4

Mrs. Beasley Packed Her Purse

VIOLET NESDOLY

Fearing things would just get worse
Mrs. Beasley packed her purse:

Cell phone, blanket, tire jack,
A map so she could make it back.

Rain umbrella, steaks and fries,
Drops and goggles for her eyes.

Gloves and flippers, skates and socks,
Lotion for the chicken pox.

Pound of breath mints, whistle, mace,
Sunscreen to protect her face.

Shovel, ladder, protein bar
A plastic cover for the car.

A barbecue, a four-inch book,
A frying pan so she could cook.

A deck of cards, a game of chess;
Her handbag really was a mess,

Prepared for all she could foresee,
Any eventuality.

But worse it got, and most unfunny—
She left her credit cards and money.

*Life is either a
daring adventure
or nothing.*

HELEN KELLER

The Flight of the Thunderbird

PATRICIA CENA EVANS

My mother has great faith in God, a faith often evident in her vehicular adventures. Having to take the driver's test annually each August, she starts praying in January that she passes. And each January, I start praying that she doesn't.

It's not that I don't want her to drive or be independent. It's just that her eyesight, hearing, sense of direction, and reflexes simply aren't the swiftest in the west anymore. Yet Mom has always resolutely believed otherwise—until the flight of her Thunderbird, that is.

At eighty-six years old, standing four-foot-nine, my Italian mother's brain is simultaneously sharp as a tack and stubborn as a mule. Nevertheless, she hasn't quite grasped the revelation that I have grown children of my own, and has likewise resisted my arguments that she shouldn't be driving anymore. Only God is powerful enough to pull off that kind of persuasion.

At age seventy-six, Mom drove her twenty-year-old Mustang forty miles on the freeway to her dying sister's house every day for three years. Arguments ensued about her cruising with the semis in rush-hour traffic. She'd shrug her shoulders, shake her pretty white hair around, and justify the daily trip by stating, "I just say a prayer when I put my key in the lock and the Good Lord takes care of me!" She had absolutely no doubt in her mind that Jesus would protect her, surrounding her beloved Mustang. And when the old horse finally died, she traded it in for a brand-new Thunderbird, but kept her standard pre-ignition prayer.

"So!" Mom shouted with delightful anticipation from her gurney in the ER. "When are we going to look for a new car?"

"Never," I pronounced slowly, trying to hold back both my anger and laughter at the same time. "I heard what the policeman *and* the fireman *and* the paramedic *and* the ambulance driver all had to say. What happened out there?"

"Oh, I'm fine! I was coming home from the doctor's office and got a little lost, that's all. It was getting dark and I didn't see the car. Those stupid air bags went off and I got out of the car so I could breathe, walked to the sidewalk, and waited for someone. The policeman came—a very nice young man. He asked if I was wearing my seat belt. I told him I couldn't tell a lie and no, I wasn't. That's all, no biggie."

"'No biggie'? Mom, you totaled three cars! Your Thunderbird literally took flight into a parked car, which dominoed into another parked car, demolishing all three!"

"I don't know what you're talking about," she replied, using the blithely dogmatic tone she always uses when I talk too fast and she doesn't understand. "All I know is that I don't have a car now, and I have to go to church! So, when are we going car shopping?"

I felt sorry for her. She obviously wasn't hurt, not even a complaint about a sore neck or back. And it wasn't her pride she was worried about—"pride comes before a fall" had long been a favorite saying of hers.

"'No biggie'? Mom, you totaled three cars! Your Thunderbird literally took flight into a parked car, which dominoed into another parked car, demolishing all three!"

But her freedom was gravely at stake. And I sensed that for the first time she knew she would never drive again, but she was going down fighting.

"Mom, your driving days are over," I said solemnly, quietly. But she hadn't missed a day of church in years, and she wasn't about to start now. And so my words fell on deaf ears.

"Oh, don't be silly. I didn't hurt anyone!"

"Mom, listen to me. They are not going to give you your license back. You had a restricted one, remember? No driving at night, you were supposed to wear your glasses, and you admitted to the cop that you weren't wearing your seat belt. You totaled three cars—did I mention that? Do you really think you're going to get your driver's license back?" I was suddenly acutely aware of our role reversal and noted how different it was to tell your mother she can't have the car keys than to tell your teenager.

"But I have to go to church!" she yelled loudly enough for the entire ER to hear.

"How do you feel, ma'am?" the ER doctor asked abruptly.

"Fine, fine. Not a thing hurts! Just my poor car is damaged." *Mom, do you understand the word "totaled"?* I wanted to scream.

"Your chest X-rays are negative and your blood pressure is better than mine. You've just got a little burn from the air bags on your chest. You can take Tylenol for pain. You're free to go home." After thanking and kissing the "nice young male nurse" on the cheek, she dressed herself and practically skipped out of the ER, pulling me along by my hand behind her. I was having difficulty remembering just how old I actually was.

That was four months ago. She has surrendered to the fact that she won't drive again, and I think she's secretly relieved that she never has to take another driver's test. Never having complained once about pain, Mom has not missed a day of church. (Our family has come together to see that Grams gets to church on time each week.)

"How can you not hurt after that accident, Mom?" I asked more than once after that fateful night.

"I just said a prayer that the Good Lord would protect me, and He did."

As her Thunderbird took flight that evening, she wasn't trusting in chariots—or Ford Motor Company—but in God. Because of her undoubting faith, He protected her yet again. Both of our prayers were answered—hers for protection, mine for taking her off the road. And as her prayers change from *Lord, please let me pass my driver's test* to *Lord, please get me to church*, I have no doubt He will stay faithful.

They say the older we get, the more we become like our mothers. As a teenager, I was horrified at this maxim. But now that I'm an adult, I hope I will be just like my mom—a woman who will leave a legacy of undoubting faith in her Lord Jesus. ⬡

As her Thunderbird took flight that evening, she wasn't trusting in chariots—or Ford Motor Company—but in God.

SOME TRUST IN CHARIOTS, OTHERS IN HORSES,
BUT WE TRUST THE LORD OUR GOD.

PSALM 20:7

Strength, rest, guidance, grace, help, sympathy, love —all from God to us! What a list of blessings!

E. STENBOCK

Away from it All

MARK 1:35

If you read through the four Gospels, you can't help but notice how people—and crowds—were drawn to Jesus. If He went up a hill to pray alone, the crowds would gather below awaiting His return (Luke 4:42). If He jumped into a boat to slip off to the other side of a lake, word of His movements would race Him to the other side (Matthew 14:13). He interacted non-stop with military officers, widows, children, the seriously ill, the demon-possessed, religious leaders, close friends, prophets, and sinners.

At the beginning of His ministry at age thirty, despite having so much to do in such a short amount of time for His Father in heaven, Jesus pulled away from everyone to spend forty days in the wilderness to pray and fast. While alone, Jesus was tested three times by Satan, but each time answered the challenge with Scripture and a profound sense of His purpose in life (Matthew 4:1-11).

Again, at the end of His earthly life, Jesus pulled away from the crowds to pray alone in the Garden of Gethsemane (Mark 14:35-36). It was there, with the agony of the cross just before Him, that He reaffirmed His most earnest desire: "Not My will, but Yours, be done" (Luke 22:42 NKJV).

If Jesus Christ sought solitude and quiet, how much more important is it for us? We can come to the end of the day—or week or even month—and discover that we made no time at all to be alone with God. Television, radio, meetings, chores, and a cacophony of other "noises" crowd out prayer and silent reflection.

If it feels like the tangles and stresses and mishaps of life are closing in on you, maybe it's time to follow Jesus' example and pull away for a while, taking time to remember what's most important. The good news is that you don't have to take a forty-day trip to the desert to be alone with God. Solitude is just a matter of giving yourself a little quiet time.

O God, You are my God;
Early will I seek You;
My soul thirsts for You;
My flesh longs for You
In a dry and thirsty land
Where there is no water.

PSALM 63:1 NKJV

God's Promises for Daily Tangles

God will...

Take on your life's battles

The Lord says this to you: "Don't be afraid or discouraged because of this large army. The battle is not your battle, it is God's."

2 CHRONICLES 20:15

Help you face problems

So we can be sure when we say, "I will not be afraid, because the Lord is my helper."

HEBREWS 13:6

Give you peace

The Lord gives strength to his people; the Lord blesses his people with peace.

PSALM 29:11

Give you everything you need
*My God will use his wonderful riches in
Christ Jesus to give you everything you need.*

PHILIPPIANS 4:19

Use your circumstances to bless you
*We know that in everything God works
for the good of those who love him.*

ROMANS 8:28

Guide your life
*I am the Lord your God, who teaches
you to do what is good, who leads
you in the way you should go.*

ISAIAH 48:17

Give you joy and strength
*Don't be sad, because the joy
of the Lord will make you strong.*

NEHEMIAH 8:10

A Prayer for Patience and Faith

Dear Heavenly Father,
Everything's falling apart today, Lord!
I pray that You would lead me beside still
waters, that You would bring me a sense
of calm and peace in the midst of chaos.
Lord, please give me a fresh perspective
on the challenges I'm facing—and help
me face them with faith in You.

Thank You for Your presence
in the middle of crazy days.

WINDY DAYS

Adversity is like a strong wind. It tears away
from us all but the things that cannot be torn,
so that we see ourselves as we really are.

ARTHUR GOLDEN

I didn't think it would ever happen. After years of fighting, Dad and I finally started getting along, and for the first time that I can even remember, we're really talking.

The doctor just told him that his PSI count is way too high and that they need him to come in for a biopsy.

When life isn't fair, when irony replaces simple joy as the prevailing mood, we sometimes just have to trust God to see us through the storm. "Sharing the Wealth" and "Perfect Timing" are wonderful examples of simple trust and are sure to keep you company as you ride out the wind and rain.

WE KNOW THAT IN EVERYTHING GOD WORKS
FOR THE GOOD OF THOSE WHO LOVE HIM.

ROMANS 8:28

Although the world is full of suffering, it is full also of the overcoming of it.

HELEN KELLER

Sharing the Wealth

JAN ECKLES

At age thirty-two, my world turned dark. A hereditary disease of the retina robbed my sight, and with it my optimism and joy. But the episodes of anguish and despair ended when Jesus came into my life. The warmth of His love dispelled the chill of my misfortune. He gave me eyes to see my world with a new and different perception.

One of my bitterest resentments when I became blind was losing my freedom to drive to the mall. Looking back now, I feel a hint of embarrassment at the rather shallow way I set my priorities—back then, if I had the choice to spend my time shopping or meditating on God's Word, I knew I'd be grabbing my car keys in no time.

That all changed with Jesus in my life. All my activities now hold a different value. If a friend calls and invites me to go to the mall, I usually accept. But, unlike before, I go for the company and friendship, not for the deals.

Every time my friends and I go out for a shopping day, I come home with stories to tell. I forewarn them that shopping with a blind person is quite an adventure and that they should prepare to be a little bit shocked—and a lot amused.

Sales clerks often ask my friend questions like, "Do you think she likes the blue or green sweater?" Why would they direct the question to my friend when I'm standing right next to her? Other clerks ask me a question so loud I could hear them even if I were standing in the parking lot. I guess they think I might be able to see if they spoke a little louder. Or maybe when they learn I'm blind, they assume my hearing is gone too!

I forewarn my friends that shopping with a blind person is quite an adventure and that they should prepare to be a little bit shocked—and a lot amused.

But it's not too hard to find the humor in our shopping experiences, and I'm careful never to miss an opportunity to express my appreciation for any help clerks and shoppers give.

I don't use a guide dog. And when accompanied by someone, I don't use a cane. Consequently, embarrassing moments often slip in without warning, but they usually add a little spice to our day and give us a good laugh later on. On one occasion, a good friend left me standing by the checkout counter of a clothing store. "Wait for me here," she instructed, and went off to look for an item for me. I obeyed her orders and stood silently beside the counter.

Moments later, in the midst of the shoppers' busy chatter, I heard, "Can I help you?"

"Yes, I'm looking for a black skirt, size four petite," I responded to the friendly salesclerk.

"Yes, ma'am."

"Do you know if you have that size in this department?" I asked.

"Yes, ma'am,"

"Would you be able to find it for me? I'm visually impaired," I requested.

When she answered, "I'll go ahead and transfer you to that department," I realized that she had been talking on the phone—not to me. *Thank goodness I can't see the expressions of these ladies around me!* I thought with relief, pretending that nothing strange had just occurred. My friend and I giggled about it all the way home.

As I trained myself to see the humor and fun in the world around me, I also made efforts to teach my small sons to see the lighter side of life—efforts which sometimes came back to haunt me. Each night, I'd visit their bedrooms, one by one, talk with them a bit, pray with them, and kiss them goodnight. One evening, as I walked into our five-year-old's room, I noticed it was quieter than usual. I tiptoed, felt for the bed, reached for the pillow, followed it, and bent over to kiss his cheek.

I jerked back—something was different. Knowing I'd be kissing him goodnight, he'd gone under his covers head first, and his wiggling feet were on his pillow.

He answered, "That's not hair spray. That's the jewelry cleaner we bought at the mall."

The simplest of daily tasks can be a source of entertainment for both me and my husband. One morning, as I got ready for a Toastmaster's meeting, I put on my makeup and fixed my hair (a simple task for me after twenty years of practicing without sight—or so I thought). I took extra care because, on this particular morning, I'd be giving a speech. I grabbed the spray bottle and liberally squirted my hair, but noticed that my coif felt wet rather than stiff as it usually does. I sprayed some more, hoping that would do the trick.

But it still felt wet. I walked into the bedroom and asked with curiosity, "Honey, what hair spray is this?"

Half asleep, he answered, "That's not hair spray. That's the jewelry cleaner we bought at the mall."

Speechless and somewhat panicked, I heard his groggy but well-intentioned words of reassurance, "Honey, don't worry—it's only a little ammonia."

I stopped for a moment, evaluated the situation, shrugged, and—ammonia head and all—went to give my speech. And to my surprise, I received a first-place ribbon. Perhaps the laughter that erupted from the audience when I told my hair spray story gave me extra points.

Why do I choose to laugh when it seems more logical to mope and complain? The answer is simple: My joy is in the Lord, not in circumstances. Like a treasure box, I store in my heart the jewels of God's reassurance, the rubies of His promises, the emeralds of His comfort, and the diamonds of His love. I choose to share this wealth with those whose bank accounts of laughter and joy may, for the moment, have a negative balance. ⭘

THEN I WILL LEAD THE BLIND ALONG A WAY THEY NEVER KNEW;
I WILL GUIDE THEM ALONG PATHS THEY HAVE NOT KNOWN.
I WILL MAKE THE DARKNESS BECOME LIGHT FOR THEM,
AND THE ROUGH GROUND SMOOTH. THESE ARE THE THINGS
I WILL DO; I WILL NOT LEAVE MY PEOPLE.

ISAIAH 42:16

They Said It

How can something bother you if you won't let it?

TERRI GUILLEMETS

Birds sing after a storm; why shouldn't people
feel as free to delight in whatever remains to them?

ROSE F. KENNEDY

Pain is inevitable. Suffering is optional.

M. KATHLEEN CASEY

You'll never find a better sparring partner than adversity.

WALT SCHMIDT

God uses suffering as a whetstone, to make men sharp with.

HENRY WARD BEECHER

I can't change the direction of the wind, but I can
adjust my sails to always reach my destination.

JIMMY DEAN

A Real Home

NANCY B. GIBBS

She was a single mother with a five-year-old son and piles of bills. Just to stay afloat, she rented a musty, cramped camper at a local RV park.

She was embarrassed and discouraged by her surroundings. She cringed one day as she overheard someone ask her little boy if he wished they had a real home. But her grimace was replaced with a tear and a smile when she heard him give this reply:

"We do have a real home; we just don't have a house to put it in." ⬢

The Lord is close to everyone who prays to him, to all who truly pray to him.

PSALM 145:18

Four Steps to Healthy Hair

One of the best ways to ward off bad hair days and keep hair looking great is to keep it healthy.

- Eat well. You've heard it before—lots of green, leafy vegetables, fruits, lean protein, and water for optimum health. But good-for-you foods are good for your hair as well. So eat your vegetables!

- Shampoo regularly. Lather up several times a week to rid your hair of excess oil and pollutants. Use a separate conditioner if you need extra moisture.

- Be gentle. Using a brush on wet hair can cause breakage, so instead, use a wide-toothed comb to detangle your just-washed mane.

- Don't dry out. Try to air-dry your hair as often as possible. When you do use a blow-dryer, make sure you apply product to serve as a buffer against the heat.

Be good to your hair, and it will be strong, healthy, and vibrant no matter what the winds may blow your way! ✿

God even knows how many hairs are on your head.

MATTHEW 10:30

Shared joy is a double joy;
shared sorrow is half a sorrow.

SWEDISH PROVERB

You're Never Too Old for a Slumber Party

When life's stiff breezes start to feel more like a tornado, there's nothing better than friends and family for making life fun again. Why not throw a slumber party for you and your family? Shove aside the couch and coffee table and stock up on pretzels and hot chocolate, and let the fun begin! Play board games, tell jokes, watch a DVD—maybe even sleep a little. Most importantly, love on the people closest to you and let them love on you.

Joke Break

Who says good jokes can't be corny? Whether these jokes make you chuckle or roll your eyes, they just might take the sting out of your windy day.

How does the man in the moon cut his hair?
Eclipse it.

If you see the handwriting on the wall, what does that mean?
That there's a child in the family.

Why are giraffes so slow to apologize?
It takes them a long time to swallow their pride.

*Laughter gives us distance.
It allows us to step back
from an event, deal with it,
and then move on.*

BOB NEWHART

A Guide for Life

BARBARA MARSHAK

I was about to face the most daunting challenge of my life. I was days from relocating back to my home state of Minnesota, days from having divorce papers signed, and days from transitioning to single parenthood with my two small daughters.

But there was one thing calling out to me before I officially said goodbye to Tennessee: I'd always wanted to really experience Mammoth Cave a few miles north of the Kentucky state line. Thousands of tourists wandered through a portion of the cave each year aided by lights, handrails, and man-made steps. I too had taken those tours, but I longed to try the audacious Wild Cave Tour, a journey through the deepest caves that was not for the average tourist. Something in me was dying to be challenged, to accomplish some wild feat before I started my new life.

Something in me was dying to be challenged, to accomplish some wild feat before I started my new life.

I'd never quite managed to talk anyone into going with me—until my niece, Sally, arrived to help me pack. Ten years younger than me, she'd always looked up to her "favorite aunt," and despite her fear of heights, she agreed to accompany me on the cave tour.

Securing a tour buddy was a feat in itself, really. The stringent requirements for the five-mile trek should have scared off a non-athlete like me. One particularly interesting restriction dictated that no part of the body be larger than forty-four inches around. Cave experience was preferred, but not required. Only twelve participants were allowed at a time.

Sally and I arrived at Mammoth Cave wearing our best jeans, coordinating sweatshirts, tennies, and colorful gardening gloves. I can only imagine what dread must have crossed our guide's mind as we, the only two females, converged with ten experienced spelunkers at the visitor's center.

The guide handed out kneepads and helmets, and a bus took us to one of the cave entrances, where we descended roughly a mile underground. Despite the stifling August heat and humidity outside, the cave temperature remained a cool fifty-four degrees. No handrails. No electric lights. Just the barren, raw earth.

The only source of light now came from the small lamps affixed to our helmets. My helmet was much too big, and my light flashed in every direction except forward. Finally I stuffed one of my garden gloves inside to hold it in place while I tried to keep up with the others. Oftentimes there were two or three corridors to choose from with immediate twists and turns. Once, I lagged behind a short distance and lost sight of the lamps ahead of me. How easy it would be to get lost—the thought sent a chill down my spine, and I quickened my steps.

How easy it would be to get lost—the thought sent a chill down my spine, and I quickened my steps.

We made our way through the caves, copying our guide's every move. When he dropped to his hands and knees, we did the same. When he slithered on his belly, we slithered right behind him. When he precariously straddled a deep, dark opening, we cautiously mirrored his every move.

At one point along a winding passageway, the guide stopped momentarily. "Okay, turn off your lamps," he advised. One by one the lamps switched off and we were swallowed up in instant darkness. An eerie chill fell over the hushed group as the guide shared legends of lost cave goers.

Somehow the sea of blackness thickened with each story.

Now back on course, we reached a section of the corridor with an eight-foot drop in the center. We straddled the chasm without too much difficulty until we reached the end, where it dropped even deeper. At this point, Sally's fear of heights took hold and she froze in place until the guide crawled underneath her and coaxed her forward, step by step.

As the day progressed, I could feel my muscles tiring. At the end of the chasm, we needed to jump to a ridge along the cave wall. Second to last in line, I watched everyone else make it safely across. As I jumped forward, my right foot landed on the edge of the boulder, but started to slip in the dirt. I began to slide backward, but stopped when a sturdy and unexpected hand landed on my back, pushing me forward. Together, the guy behind me and I landed safely.

Soon it was time to maneuver through what was affectionately christened the Mole Hole, an awkward Z-shaped passage. I made it through without problem, immediately crawling down the opposite wall into the Snowball Dining Room. One by one, each person maneuvered the crevice until one young man with a fairly broad chest started through. Already stripped down to his T-shirt, his chest became pressed against the narrow opening and he couldn't maneuver his body forward or backward. In a word, he was stuck.

Panic consumed him immediately, and he began hyperventilating. Those on my side could see his petrified expression. Our guide, however, remained completely calm. He told the young man to relax, take deeps breaths, and release the air. Slowly, his chest compressed and he was able to squeeze through. His deep relief showed in his scratched, red face.

At the end of the six-hour journey, covered in rusty, red Kentucky dirt from head to toe, Sally and I left the cool climate of the cave and stepped into the muggy afternoon, immediately collapsing on a park bench. We'd survived! Somehow we'd overcome each obstacle we encountered.

In the following weeks and months, I faced more obstacles. New and different challenges were presented daily as I set about the task of finding a job and a place to live, and I sometimes felt as inexperienced as I had in the caves. Could a stay-at-home mom without a college degree make it on her own?

Step by step, I learned to listen to God as I made important decisions. The familiarity of my hometown set the backdrop for a wonderful support system of friends and family; only God knew how important that would be. Next, I found a job in my daughters' school—God's way of keeping me close to my girls throughout the day. Then I purchased a home only blocks from the school.

As my trust deepened, so did my faith. I found myself embracing God's nearness and strength, thankful for His guiding presence. He is, after all, the guide I need for life.

MY GOD BRIGHTENS THE DARKNESS AROUND ME.

PSALM 18:28

Against the Wind and Waves

MATTHEW 8:23-27

Wild wind. Water everywhere that seems to have a mind of its own. We've all experienced that feeling of having no control over what's happening and no idea how things will turn out. When Jesus' disciples encountered a storm, they experienced that same feeling of panic. But with only a few simple words to them—"Why are you afraid? You don't have enough faith"—and even fewer words directed to the storm, He calmed the storm and His disciples' hearts.

Jesus' response to storms reminds us of a couple simple lessons for our own lives—

- Storms are no respecters of persons. Everyone—the good, the bad, and the pretty—will face adversity. If Jesus, the only perfect person ever to live, faced storms, with His true trials ahead, then we should expect adversity too. As He put it, God "sends rain to those who do right and to those who do wrong" (Matthew 5:45).

- Storms can't defeat us; it is only when we give in to fear that the battle is lost. Franklin Delano Roosevelt said: "The only thing we have to fear is fear itself." Paul reminds us that "God did not give us a spirit that makes us afraid but a spirit of power and love and self-control" (2 Timothy 1:7).

With faith and trust in God, we can weather storms with grace and poise. No, none of us desire adversity and challenges in our lives, but we can experience a supernatural strength and calm when we declare with Paul: "We know that in everything God works for the good of those who love him" (Romans 8:28). ⬢

JESUS STOOD UP AND COMMANDED
THE WIND AND SAID TO THE WAVES,
"QUIET! BE STILL!" THEN THE WIND
STOPPED, AND IT BECAME
COMPLETELY CALM.

MARK 4:39

God's Promises for Difficult Days

God will...

Hear your prayers

When I was in danger, I called to the Lord, and he answered me.

JONAH 2:2

Use troubles to make you stronger

My brothers and sisters, when you have many kinds of troubles, you should be full of joy, because you know that these troubles test your faith, and this will give you patience.

JAMES 1:2-3

Be with you

When you pass through the waters, I will be with you. When you cross rivers, you will not drown. When you walk through fire, you will not be burned, nor will the flames hurt you.

ISAIAH 43:2

Restore you and guide you
*Then I will lead the blind along a way they
never knew; I will guide them along paths
they have not known. I will make the darkness
become light for them, and the rough ground smooth.
These are the things I will do; I will not leave my people.*

ISAIAH 42:16

Give you joy as you trust Him
We rejoice in him, because we trust his holy name.

PSALM 33:21

Be a refuge in times of trouble
*God is our protection and our strength.
He always helps in times of trouble.*

PSALM 46:1

A Prayer for Grace and Wisdom

Dear Heavenly Father,

*My life doesn't feel very stable right now.
Lord, You know the things I'm facing. I need
Your counsel today. I need Your strength and
peace. Lord, I pray that You would come beside
me and help me remember that You're there.*

*Thank You for Your goodness. Thank You
that Your love and grace are enough to
see me through the darkest of times.*

RUNNING LATE AGAIN

The Law of Waiting: For each minute you are running late, the chances of being stuck behind a slow school bus or being caught by a train at a crossing increases exponentially. Direct correlation: When you are running on time, it is entirely likely you will be pulled over for speeding.

AUTHOR UNKNOWN

I was playing a trivia game with a group of friends and can't believe I came up with the answer to the question: "What is the capital of Mongolia?" It was like a flash from the sky. I even knew how to spell "Ulaanbaatar." I was so impressed with myself.

The only problem was I didn't come up with the answer until two hours after the game was over.

Ever shown up at the right place, but at the wrong time? Or maybe the only week you got to church early was when you forgot to turn the clock back for the end of Daylight Savings Time.

After reading "Don't Forget to Pray, Mommy" and "A Bigger Heart," you'll know you're not alone in being a day late and a dollar short—but with a smile, there are always better days ahead!

AS PRESSURE AND STRESS BEAR DOWN ON ME,
I FIND JOY IN YOUR COMMANDS.

PSALM 119:143 NLT

*If your day is hemmed
in prayer, it is less likely
to come unstitched.*

ANONYMOUS

Don't Forget to Pray, Mommy

AUTUMN J. CONLEY

As a single mom working one and a half jobs just to keep the lights on and a little gas in the car, my life often feels like a three-ring circus. I don't mind the circus so much, but trying to ringmaster all those rings at once can make my head spin.

On one of these manic, crazy-busy days, my bright seven-year-old reminded me that the one thing that could have taken the sting out of the rush-bug was the first thing eliminated from my to-do list.

I had left the office in a hurry, trying to escape my ever-expanding inbox with some shred of sanity. I sped home, my mind frantically occupied with dinner to be made, newsletters to be typed, laundry to be done, posters to be created, homework to be reviewed, and lunches to be packed.

My daughter came wandering to the car when I got to the sitter's. I remember my own mom accusing me of being "slower than Moses." I was convinced Moses could move faster than my daughter even if he was on crutches. As she piled her backpack, her muddy shoes, and herself into the backseat, I sighed, revved the engine, and said, "Mommy's in a hurry. Come on," in a frustrated huff. I suppose it would have taken too much precious time to say hi before I started grumbling.

"You're always in a hurry," she mumbled, looking out the window. I felt bad. But still I kept on rushing and huffing and sighing.

By ten that night, I was finally able to get around to prepping my daughter for bed—lucky her. I just knew that long after she had drifted into sleep with her stuffed hippo beneath her fluffy pink quilt, I'd still be awake, busily attending to details. I tucked her in, kissed her hastily on the forehead, and said goodnight.

She stopped me in my rushed tracks as I flicked off the Strawberry Shortcake light switch. "Mommy, make sure to say your prayers before you go to sleep," she soberly commanded. I was glad she reminded me, but embarrassed that she had to.

In my crazy task- and worry-filled day, I hadn't left room for the most important thing of all, and my daughter, as young as she was, had remembered something so much more vital than laundry and meetings and oil changes and spelling lists.

God tells us to "be still." I think He tells us this because He knows that our lives are not still, and it takes some effort on our part. It isn't always easy to set aside time to pray and commit my fast-paced life to God. But being still and soaking up His provision of wisdom and guidance is worth every effort. And, thankfully, even if I forget to put Him on my agenda, He always puts me on His. ✿

THE THING YOU SHOULD WANT MOST IS GOD'S KINGDOM AND DOING WHAT GOD WANTS. THEN ALL THESE OTHER THINGS YOU NEED WILL BE GIVEN TO YOU.

MATTHEW 6:33-34

> *God will do the right thing at the right time. And what a difference that makes! Since you know that His provision is timely, you can enjoy the present.*
>
> **MAX LUCADO**

Psalm 136

MICHELLE TELLING

Psalm 136 tells us that whatever happened yesterday, whatever happens today or tomorrow, God's love endures forever.

Someone left the freezer door open yesterday, and now I have boxes of soggy fish sticks and peas, melted ice cream, and half a cow that needs to be cooked up within twenty-four hours.

His love endures forever.

The ironing pile is overflowing onto the floor.

His love endures forever.

I finally managed to start on the ironing pile, but I burned my husband's favorite shirt.

His love endures forever.

Grandma mercifully took us out for lunch after church, but my four-year-old stood up on the chair in the restaurant and threw up all over the table.

His love endures forever.

I forgot to pick my oldest up from school this afternoon, and even though a kind neighbor brought him home for me, I feel like a terrible mother.

His love endures forever.

The children have chicken pox, I have a report due at work, Grandma and Granddad have gone on vacation (not that I blame them), and I can't get hold of a babysitter.

His love endures forever.

The dishwasher has decided it needs a break, last night's

dishes are still on the counter, and we have company coming for Sunday lunch.

His love endures forever.

Someone stood in some dog poo before we hopped in the car for a four-hour trip through the pouring rain.

His love endures forever.

We have finally managed to get away on vacation, but it started raining yesterday and hasn't stopped since.

His love endures forever.

We return home, and—surprise, surprise—my ironing pile is exactly where I left it: overflowing onto the floor.

His love endures forever.

Next time your life gets frantic, remember that God's love really does endure forever. Because of His love for you, you know that He wants the very best for you and will help you through whatever comes your way—and there are no ironing piles in heaven.

They Said It

Our real work is prayer.
What good is the cold iron of our
frantic little efforts unless first we heat
it in the furnace of our prayer?
Only heat will diffuse heat.

MOTHER MARIBEL

Some of the secret joys of living are not found
by rushing from point A to point B, but by
inventing some imaginary letters along the way.

DOUGLAS PAGELS

I try to take one day at a time,
but sometimes several days attack me at once.

JENNIFER YANE

The fashion-wise woman doesn't run
herself frantic trying to keep up
with the latest rage, fad, or craze.

LORETTA YOUNG

Happy Thoughts

ESTHER BAILEY

Between personnel problems and cranky patients, Amy experienced considerable stress on her job as a nurse. Sometimes her frustration went home with her.

Although Amy tried to spare the children from her moods, four-year-old Brad took notice that Mom didn't always feel very happy. One evening, before she left for the night shift at the hospital, the child seemed sad as he hugged her goodbye. Suddenly his face brightened and he said, "Mom, while you're at work, think happy thoughts."

With a smile Mom said, "Thanks, Brad. I'll do that." That night she thought positively—for Brad. But to her surprise, she found the evening much less strenuous and painful than usual. And so she decided to think happy thoughts at work and at home, for Brad and for herself. ⬡

S.O.S.

BONNIE COMPTON HANSON

Dear beautician, hear my plea:
This is a real emergency!
How much beauty can you slip
To me for twenty bucks, plus tip?

Hair 911

- To fix "I overslept" hair maladies in a hurry, wake up your roots with a blow dryer and lightly apply styling product. If your hair has retained its sleep position and refuses to cooperate, there's nothing wrong with putting it up—pull your hair into a ponytail holder, then pull it through again and stop halfway, leaving a few loose pieces.

- For midday emergencies, keep a hair first-aid kit with you (seriously). Include a small mist bottle of water (water will reactivate your styling product—just mist your hair and reshape), a travel-size hair spray or gel, and a clip to pull your hair into a last-resort, but still cute updo.

- If your well-coifed locks have fallen flat at the end of the day, but you don't have time to redo your do, try running your hair under a blow-dryer, or even a restroom hand-dryer if you're away from home. If your hair tends to get frizzy, wet your hands and scrunch your hair as you dry. ⚙

Take rest; a field
that has rested gives
a bountiful crop.

OVID

Double Feature

After a full week of chasing the clock, you need a break! Pick out one or two movies, pop some popcorn, and sit the kids or some lucky friends down on the couch for a film festival. After the films, engage in a little discussion on a few items. Did the movie end the way you wanted it to? Were you surprised? Were the events realistic? Fantastical? Exciting? Boring? Were the actors believable? Were any of your favorite actors in this movie?

Watch for continuity errors. Quote your favorite lines. Pick out awards for worst costume, goofiest line, best hair, most beautiful scenery. Whatever you do, don't rush—this is your vacation from having to hurry. ⬢

Joke Break

The best thing about these jokes might be that they don't take too long to read, which means you won't be later than you already are!

What do you get if you cross a pig and a red light?
A stop swine.

What is the laziest shoe?
A loafer.

What happens to a deer when an archer shoots at it and misses?
It has an arrow escape.

The man who doesn't
relax and hoot a few hoots
voluntarily, now and then,
is in great danger
of hooting hoots and
standing on his head
for the edification
of the pathologist
and trained nurse,
a little later on.

ELBERT HUBBARD

A Bigger Heart

LUKE 19:1-10

If you grew up attending church, maybe you remember singing a song about a small man named Zacchaeus: *Zacchaeus was a wee little man, oh, a wee little man was he. So he climbed up in a sycamore tree for the Lord he wanted to see.*

We don't know a lot about Zacchaeus' background, though we do know he was a small man—but not just because of his height. Like the Grinch from Dr. Seuss, what was truly small was his heart. A corrupt tax collector, he stole from his own people on behalf of the Romans, and as a result, they despised him and he despised them.

But apparently, deep in his soul, Zacchaeus wanted something more in his life. He didn't want more money. He wanted to love and to be loved. That all became possible when Jesus came along.

Between his height and his social troubles, Zacchaeus probably missed out on a lot of things. But one thing he made sure he didn't miss was a chance to see Jesus—even if it meant climbing the nearest sycamore tree to catch a glimpse of Him.

He opened his home to Jesus—and those he once despised. Unlike the rich young ruler who loved money more than people, Zacchaeus also opened his pocketbook and paid back even more than he had stolen. Most of all, he opened his heart to the life-changing power of God's love. And just like the Grinch, his heart grew three sizes in an instant.

If you're running late today, take a cue from Zacchaeus and do whatever it takes to have an encounter with Jesus. The day will certainly get better as a result. ⬡

> LOVE THE LORD YOUR GOD WITH ALL YOUR HEART,
> ALL YOUR SOUL, AND ALL YOUR MIND. THIS IS
> THE FIRST AND MOST IMPORTANT COMMAND.
>
> **MATTHEW 22:37-38**

God's Promises for Frantic Days

Be your refuge
He is my rock and my salvation.
He is my defender; I will not be defeated.

PSALM 62:2

Give you strength and never leave you
We are persecuted, but God does not leave us.
We are hurt sometimes, but we are not destroyed.

2 CORINTHIANS 4:9

Refresh you
He gives me new strength.
He leads me on paths that are right
for the good of his name.

PSALM 23:3

Guide you
In all your ways acknowledge Him,
And He shall direct your paths.

PROVERBS 3:6 NKJV

Give you peace
I leave you peace; my peace I give you.
I do not give it to you as the world does.
So don't let your hearts be troubled or afraid.

JOHN 14:27

Help you when you're tired
The Lord helps those who have been defeated
and takes care of those who are in trouble.

PSALM 145:14

A Prayer for Peace and Perspective

Dear Heavenly Father,

So many things are demanding my attention right now, and I'm just not at the top of my game today. Lord God, thank You that You know what I need and care about the details of my life. Help me remember that life is more than food, the body more than clothes—help me remember that seeking You is the best thing I can do with my life.

Thank You for the peace You offer me, Lord. Help me rest in that peace today.

UNEXPECTED "SURPRISES"

Every survival kit should include a sense of humor.

AUTHOR UNKNOWN

"Hi, honey. I have good news and bad news. Which do you want first?"

"Uh-oh. Better start with the good news."

"Okay. Remember how we showed a two thousand-dollar refund from the IRS that we've been waiting for?"

"Yes."

"Well, they finally got back to us."

"So we got the check? Is that the good news?"

"Yes and no. We didn't get the check, but we finally heard from them. The bad news is we're being indicted."

Life has a way of throwing curve balls at us! Just read "Nifty Fifty" and "You Get What You Pay For."

Don't lose heart, even if you've struck out a few times. God is on your side!

THINK ABOUT THE THINGS THAT ARE GOOD AND
WORTHY OF PRAISE. THINK ABOUT THE THINGS
THAT ARE TRUE AND HONORABLE AND RIGHT AND
PURE AND BEAUTIFUL AND RESPECTED.

PHILIPPIANS 4:8

The beautiful thing about this adventure called faith is that we can count on Him never to lead us astray.

CHUCK SWINDOLL

Nifty Fifty

PATRICIA LORENZ

Come on, Mom, I'm really hungry for a big cheeseburger and fries! Can't we go out to eat?" my son, Andrew, implored.

"No. Fast food is too expensive. We've got leftover meatloaf at home," I snapped.

Lately, as my fiftieth birthday loomed just over the horizon, I'd become a money-hoarding crab.

I'd loved my forties. They were fun, energetic, and full of life.

I'd accomplished a lot during my forties. A month before I turned forty I became a single parent to my four children, but thanks to team effort and lots of prayer, we survived the next decade beautifully. I not only got the three oldest through their teenage years without too many new gray hairs, they were now college graduates living on their own and supporting themselves with interesting careers. My youngest, Andrew, was the only one still at home— a terrific high-school sophomore involved in sports and band.

My forties had been happy years, filled with meaning and purpose. But I just wasn't sure about turning fifty. The big day in October was only months away. That July, things started to go downhill.

Yes, indeed, my forties had been happy years, filled with meaning and purpose. But I just wasn't sure about turning fifty. The big day in October was only months away. That July, things started to go downhill.

The day before I left for my two-week vacation from my job at a radio station, I received a letter from the social security administration.

"I don't understand this," I blubbered to the representative on the phone after I tore open the letter.

She responded kindly, "If a minor child only has one living parent, that parent receives financial help from social security only until the child is sixteen. The child continues to receive it until he's eighteen, however."

I hung up the phone in a daze. In four months, one-third of my annual income would be gone.

Well, it was too late to cancel the vacation. My daughter in California was eagerly awaiting our arrival. And besides, I'd saved like the dickens for six months to pay for the trip. So, instead of worrying about the future, I repeated my favorite Bible verse over and over: "Depend on the Lord; trust him, and he will take care of you" (Psalm 37:5).

What I didn't know was that my financial future was just beginning its downward spiral—and most of it had to do with getting older.

The day we arrived in Oakland, a huge portion of one of my back teeth broke right off into little pieces. Three weeks later, when we returned home and the crown was put in, I had to fork over $487 to my dentist.

The next day I received a bill for the X-rays of my arthritic toe: $144.

The meager medical insurance I could afford didn't cover X-rays—of course.

That same week I noticed I was having trouble reading the fine print and sometimes even the medium print. Out of desperation I purchased a huge light for the kitchen that contained four four-foot-long fluorescent bulbs. It made cooking, bill paying, reading, and letter writing at the kitchen counter much easier for my nearly-fifty eyes. But that new light set me back $107.

Next, I made a trip to the optometrist's office. He confirmed that both my distance and close-up vision were worsening rapidly.

Naturally, I thought bitterly, as my whole physical well-being flashed before my eyes in bright neon. It screamed, *You're almost fifty, over the hill!*

The bill for the bifocals and reading glasses was $241.

That same week, I finally gave in to one too many backaches caused by the ancient desk chair in my home office. I figured that my lower back pain was just another pitfall of approaching the big five-oh—which was starting to feel like the big five-oh-no!

But once again, I repeated the verse from Psalms, stepped out in faith, and wrote a check for $105 for a superb office chair with arms and lumbar support. The day after I put that chair together, I noticed a great improvement in my back.

Well, now, at least my broken tooth was fixed, I could see near and far with my new glasses, my back didn't hurt, and my arthritic toe was feeling better. Things seemed to be looking up.

And then I sat down at my computer to add things up. All my recent dental and ophthalmic and general health care contingencies came to $1084. I was out over a thousand dollars.

> I figured that my lower back pain was just another pitfall of approaching the big five-oh—which was starting to feel like the big five-oh-no.

I took a deep breath and, once again, committed it all to the Lord.

The next day, I discovered that while we were in California, lightning had struck our TV set, rendering it completely useless. I myself could easily do without a TV, but Andrew often brought his friends to our family room to watch movies. So that week I wrote out another check for a good secondhand TV: $250.

Things were getting out of hand. First my income was going down by a third, and then suddenly there were all these unexpected bills! I wasn't just getting "over the hill" age-wise—I was careening down and out of control, financially as well as physically.

And so I prayed. *Lord, please give my guardian angel a nudge! I need a little help down here. Thank You, Lord, for providing for my son and me.* And of course I ended the prayer with "my" verse from the Psalms.

A few days later while I was still wallowing in self-pity over my impending birthday, I received a letter from a publisher. As I opened the letter, a check tumbled out. The year before, I'd written a few short daily devotionals for their annual book, but I'd already been paid for my work the previous spring.

The letter explained that in honor of their twentieth year of publication, they'd turned the distribution of the book over to a larger publisher who expected sales to skyrocket. The original publisher was sharing the advance on the royalties with all the writers of the book.

My share was $1,338.

All I could do was nod skyward toward my guardian angel with a banana-sized grin. Then I grabbed my calculator. But even before I added the cost of the TV to my list of five "getting-older" expenses, I knew that the check I was holding would cover it all.

The bills totaled $1,334. That guardian angel of mine, the one with the math background, gave me enough money for all those expenses plus two big juicy cheeseburgers and fries to share with my son.

That night as Andrew and I chowed down at his favorite fast-food place, I said what I'd been thinking all day. "Andrew, I'm thinking turning fifty isn't so bad after all. I think my fifties are going to be the best decade yet! My guardian angel and the Lord will see to it." ⬢

THE ANGEL OF THE LORD CAMPS AROUND
THOSE WHO FEAR GOD, AND HE SAVES THEM.

PSALM 34:7

Nearly all the best things that came to me in life have been unexpected, unplanned by me.

CARL SANDBURG

They Said It

Nobody says you must laugh, but a sense of humor can
help you overlook the unattractive, tolerate the unpleasant,
cope with the unexpected, and smile through the day.

ANN LANDERS

A weed is no more than a flower in disguise.

ANONYMOUS

None of us knows what the next change is going to be,
what unexpected opportunity is just around the corner, waiting
a few months or a few years to change all the tenor of our lives.

KATHLEEN NORRIS

Oh, my friend, it's not what they take away from you that counts.
It's what you do with what you have left.

HUBERT HUMPHREY

Just because you're miserable doesn't
mean you can't enjoy your life.

ANNETTE GOODHEART

Whenever you fall, pick something up.

OSWALD AVERY

Joke Break

These jokes might be more appropriate for your six-year-old than for you. Or they might be just what you need to help you laugh about whatever the day is throwing your way.

How do you find a missing barber?
Comb the city.

How do they put out fires at the post office?
They stamp them out.

When the chicken forgot her lines in the movie,
what did Barbie, the director, do to help?
Barbie cued the chicken.

Some people,
no matter how old they get,
never lose their beauty—
they merely move it from
their faces into their hearts.

MARTIN BUXBAUM

Stranger Than Fiction

According to Guinness World Records, the title of "Hairiest Family" currently belongs to the Ramos Gomez family of Mexico. Even the Ramos Gomez women have light to medium hair on 98% of their bodies, while the men have thick, dark hair on every inch of their bodies apart from their hands and feet—including the nose and forehead. The family suffers from something called hypertrichosis, and scientists are studying their DNA for clues as to their extreme condition. Twins Larry and Danny, who work as trampoline acrobats with the circus, were reportedly offered roles in The X-Files, which they respectably turned down, not wanting to be depicted as freakish aliens. Says Larry, "I'd never cut the hair off. I'm proud to be who I am."

In the animal kingdom, the hairiness record is held by either the chinchilla or the musk ox, depending on your definition of "hairy." The chinchilla has the densest fur, with about sixty hairs in each follicle, while the musk ox coat grows the longest in the animal kingdom.

Incidentally, humans can grow hair longer than the musk ox. Case in point: Xie Qiuping of China, who holds the world record for longest hair with a mane over eighteen feet long. We have no word on whether or not she experiences bad hair days, but we would imagine so. ⬡

Count your blessings.
Once you realize how
valuable you are and how
much you have going for you,
the smiles will return,
the sun will break out,
the music will play,
and you will finally be
able to move forward the
life that God intended for
you with grace, strength,
courage, and confidence.

OG MANDINO

Pay It Forward

We so often complain when things go wrong—yet we forget to express appreciation when things go right. Next time you get a great do at the salon, as a one-time extravagant gesture, show your gratitude by leaving a larger tip than you normally do. If you usually tip 20 percent, tip 30 or maybe even 50 percent. Since they made your day, make their day! An extra ten in your stylist's hands will be much appreciated, and the act of kindness and gratitude will make you even more radiant.

*You're only as good
as your last haircut.*

FRAN LEBOWITZ

You Get What You Pay For

KIM PETERSON

The same person has cut my hair for almost twenty years, but with a hint of daring and much in trepidation, I risked a departure from custom. I had forgotten to book in advance and my stylist would be too busy to fit me in before I left for a vacation.

Then there was the postcard. "Only $2.99," it shouted when I pulled it from the mailbox. They took walk-ins and I would pay about thirteen dollars less than usual. Forsaking customer loyalty, I yielded to the enticement—I had to have a good haircut for our vacation, after all.

I drove up to the shop, handed the lady at the counter my coupon, and assessed her hairstyle. Her hair looked fine. This would go quite well, I was sure.

I drove up to the shop, handed the lady at the counter my coupon, and assessed her hairstyle. Her hair looked fine. This would go quite well, I was sure.

"Follow me," she said cheerfully as she strode to her work station and grabbed a cape.

I borrowed the book of sensible hairstyles from another customer and showed the stylist what I wanted my bangs to look like. "Do you think my bangs will work okay like that?"

"Oh, yes," she assured me. "Your hair is thick enough." She fluffed my bangs a few times, nodding her head. She whipped out a spray bottle, drenched my bangs and the ends of my just below shoulder-length hair, and began cutting.

With my glasses on the counter, my vision was limited to our blurred outlines reflected in the mirror. I sat blindly trying to gauge her movements and predict the outcome of my hair adventure.

"How short do you want these bangs?" she asked.

"Just above my brows," I responded. "They grow fast and right now I look like a horse with a wild forelock."

I slipped on my glasses. Although I had prepared myself for a less-than-perfect cut, the reality stunned me. My bangs stretched the unevenness of a second-grader's skill over a fat stripe of forehead.

She chuckled. "I don't want to cut them too short. I always hate to see little old ladies wear their bangs way above their eyebrows."

She eyed her work and pulled out a razor. The scritching sound made me cringe.

"I also hate it when people try to trim their own bangs," she added. "That uneven look reminds me of a second grader who tried to give himself a haircut."

She spun the chair around and started snipping the back.

"How much off here? You should consider wearing your hair short. Long hair and a narrow face make a person look so much older."

Squelching my immediate response to her rude comment, I suggested cutting two inches off the back. She rattled on about the virtues of short hair until she finished.

Finally, the moment of truth arrived. "There you go!" she said as she spun me back toward the mirror. "What do you think? Will that do?"

I slipped on my glasses. Although I had prepared myself for a less-than-perfect cut, the reality stunned me. My bangs stretched the unevenness of a second-grader's skill over a fat stripe of forehead.

"Yes—" I squeaked, then cleared my throat. "That will be fine." I stared again at what was left of my bangs.

"Do you like it? I can adjust anything if you'd like," the stylist offered as she began sweeping my poor hair off the floor. No way was I going to let her touch my head again.

"I'll go with this," I worded my sentence carefully to avoid lying.

She ripped the Velcro closure on the cape, releasing me. I followed her to the cash register and forked over $3.27, then tried not to run out the door as other customers stared. In my car I flipped down the mirror on the visor for another look. "Well, you get what you pay for," I soberly told my reflection.

I drove home, compulsively glancing at the top of my head in the rearview mirror. Inside my house, I clipped a bit of hair from the left side to even out some of the damage.

When my husband came home, I braced myself for his reaction. "Um, what happened?" he asked guardedly.

I explained the escapade, and we both laughed loud and long.

I endured substandard hair during our vacation, and four weeks later, my regular stylist worked me in to undo some of the damage. And four weeks after that, my hair was back to normal. I'm thinking about growing my bangs out altogether—the memories are too painful, kind of a post-traumatic hair disorder. In any case, I have vowed never to use a coupon for a haircut again. ⬢

It's not easy taking my problems one at a time when they refuse to get in line.

ASHLEIGH BRILLIANT

One Problem at a Time

SHELLEY WAKE

There were too many problems in my life to solve any one of them—it was like trying to cover up with a child's blanket. My oldest son had become increasingly hyperactive and disruptive in school, and we had two frazzled teachers and a disgruntled principal to deal with, along with several irritated parents. My youngest son, frustrated that his brother was getting all the attention, lashed out by picking fights constantly. My daughter was so rattled by all the arguing that she hardly even spoke anymore.

On top of all that, there was the demanding boss and the aging car and the house falling into disrepair. I was so bogged down with problems, I couldn't possibly see over them to spot a solution.

> My neighbor glowered across the street at my dilapidated lawn. I imagined the school principal must have had a similar look on his face as we talked on the phone—disappointed, judgmental, exasperated. I looked up at my ceiling and fought back tears.

Looking out my kitchen window on what some people evidently considered a relaxing Sunday, I caught my neighbor staring at my yard. When I'd moved in, the garden glowed with beautiful, flowering rose bushes. Now, the lawn was patchy and sparse, the roses wilting and sad. I watched as my neighbor glowered across the street at my dilapidated lawn. I imagined the school principal must have had a similar look on his face as we talked on the phone—disappointed, judgmental, exasperated. I looked up at my ceiling and fought back tears.

"It's the day of rest," I mumbled. "When do I get to rest?"

Apparently I didn't get a break today, because when I looked out the window again, my neighbor was still staring at my front yard.

I closed the blinds, sunk my head down on the kitchen table, and cried. A few minutes later, a knock shook my front door.

"Definitely not a day of rest," I mumbled.

I wiped my eyes and dragged myself to the door. I opened it and saw my neighbor, looking somewhat uncomfortable, shifting his weight from one foot to the other as he greeted me. I sighed, ready to hear a speech about how I was letting down the neighborhood, just like I was letting down my kids and their classmates and an entire generation of rose growers.

"I couldn't help but notice that your roses are dying," he said.

"Yes," I said, "the roses are dying."

"It's just that they were so beautiful."

"Yes," I sighed, "they were beautiful, I know."

"This is a tough soil," he said. "What you need to do is add some lime."

I stood there, stunned. Then I felt a little glimmer of hope.

"Really? Lime will fix it?"

"Yep," he smiled. "Easy as that."

"Thank you," I said, "I think you've just saved my roses."

I wanted to tell him that he might have just saved me. But I didn't. I just smiled and thanked him again.

"Just glad to help," he said, turning to leave.

I closed the door and went back inside. I still had three children to fix, a principal, two teachers, and several upset parents to soothe, a boss to manage, and plenty of other problems on my list. But for the first time in a long time, I didn't mind too much.

"I don't know about tomorrow," I murmured as I grabbed the car keys, "but today I'm going to save the roses."

Then I went out to buy some lime. ⬡

PEOPLE WHO DO WHAT IS RIGHT MAY HAVE MANY PROBLEMS, BUT THE LORD WILL SOLVE THEM ALL.

PSALM 34:19

Miracles Often Start Small

STAN TOLER

JOHN 6:1-14

Like all great works of God, the miracle on the mountainside started simply. It started with a small boy leaving home with a sack lunch of five small loaves and two fresh fish.

He had no idea how big this day would be.

He couldn't have understood that this would be the day when he would walk into the pages of history. He didn't know that of all Jesus' miracles, this would be the only one that all four of the Gospel writers would feel compelled to include in their accounts of Christ's life. He carried his loaves and fishes in his shoulder bag for several hours that day, completely unaware that every person he met, and thousands beyond his sight, would benefit from its contents.

And he certainly didn't know that he would experience one of the great principles of Christian living. Later, when he would offer his lunch to Jesus, he would learn the lesson of a lifetime, one that every seeker after truth must understand: Receiving is a by-product of giving.

There's nothing you or I can do to "earn" God's favor. We can't afford grace, no matter how many credit cards we have. But throughout biblical history, He has offered people an opportunity to "share in the miracle."

To blind Bartimaeus, He queried, "What do you want Me to do for you?" Bartimaeus' response to the question resulted in his sight. To the centurion, who longed for the healing of his dying servant, Jesus ordered an immediate journey back home— without a miracle in hand. But the miracle was in the journey. His faith was part of the dynamic that resulted in the healing of the servant. He has given us the privilege of seeing our commitments, small as they may be, rewarded by His unlimited supply.

And often, those commitments are born during times of calamity or uncertainty. That's when we pack up whatever loaves and fishes we have and run to meet Him. ⬢

AFTER THEY HAVE PROVED THEIR FAITH,
GOD WILL REWARD THEM WITH LIFE FOREVER.
GOD PROMISED THIS TO ALL THOSE WHO LOVE HIM.
JAMES 1:12

God's Promises for the Unexpected

Give you patience
But the Spirit produces the fruit of love,
joy, peace, patience, kindness, goodness,
faithfulness, gentleness, self-control.

GALATIANS 5:22

Never leave you
God has said, "I will never leave you; I will never forget you."

HEBREWS 13:5

Never stop loving you
The Lord's love never ends; his mercies never stop.

LAMENTATIONS 3:22

Reward your efforts at doing good
We must not become tired of doing good.
We will receive our harvest of eternal life
at the right time if we do not give up.

GALATIANS 6:9

Give you security
Those who trust the Lord are like Mount Zion,
which sits unmoved forever.

PSALM 125:1

Guard your heart
And God's peace, which is so great
we cannot understand it, will keep your
hearts and minds in Christ Jesus.

PHILIPPIANS 4:7

Be with you
With his help, one Israelite could defeat
a thousand, because the Lord your God
fights for you, as he promised to do.

JOSHUA 23:10

A Prayer of Thanks and Faith

Dear Heavenly Father,

*I know that no matter how hard I try, I can't
control everything in my life. Lord, please remind
me of Your great strength and great compassion today.
Give me the faith of Hannah and David and
Abraham, who trusted and depended on You
in the midst of the difficulties they faced.*

*Thank You that You hear me when I call to You—
You listen and have infinite patience and care
to hear my thoughts as I bring my needs
and praise before You.*

A NEW DO

The cure for boredom is curiosity.
There is no cure for curiosity.

DOROTHY PARKER

There have been some pretty tough times in my life the past four years. I have to admit that there were times I wasn't sure I'd ever get everything squared away. But I woke up this morning and realized, no, everything's not perfect, but I'm a survivor and have a good life...

Is life only about struggle, or can we hope for better days? Read "Sister Act" and "The Classics" and realize just how sweet life in God can be.

LOOK AT THE NEW THING I AM GOING TO DO. IT IS
ALREADY HAPPENING. DON'T YOU SEE IT? I WILL MAKE
A ROAD IN THE DESERT AND RIVERS IN THE DRY LAND.

ISAIAH 43:19

There are those who are so afraid of doing wrong that they seldom venture to do anything.

VAUVENARUES

Sister Act

MICHELE STARKEY

I remember my father's exact words when I told him that I was quitting my high-paying job with full benefits to open a small business franchise with my sister. "Will you have medical insurance? You've had brain surgery and you need good medical insurance."

I understood his concern. I had plenty of concern of my own, and beneath my calm demeanor, I was actually terrified. After more than twenty years in the corporate world—with full medical and dental—suddenly I would be fully responsible for my own financial future and well-being. A steady paycheck, room for advancement, corporate-paid relocations, and retirement plans were about to become a thing of my past. I was embarking on a new journey. But I wasn't going it alone—I was dragging my sister with me.

> A steady paycheck, room for advancement, corporate-paid relocations and retirement plans were about to become a thing of my past. I was embarking on a new journey. But I wasn't going it alone—I was dragging my sister with me.

We had just purchased a women's fitness franchise and incorporated under the name of "Two Sisters Women's Fitness Center." Our accountant had a little trouble with the length of our business name, but I insisted on keeping it. I was proud of the fact that we were a sister act.

The decision to leave the corporate world behind had been an easy one for me. After suffering and surviving a ruptured brain aneurysm, I figured that since I had survived brain surgery and months of treatments, I could survive small business ownership. Maybe even menopause would be a breeze compared to brain surgery.

I had a new sense of perspective. My recovery forced me to live each day one minute at a time. My pre-aneurysm self didn't know the meaning of the word *patience*. You know those people who tap their horn as soon as the light changes, impatient with drivers who don't go the instant they see green? That was me then. Now I'm the one who gets beeped at because I'm too busy watching the birds fly in formation or searching for rainbows in the clouds.

I've learned to show more compassion when dealing with people and their misfortunes. I've learned to listen to people, even risking my sister's wrath by momentarily shirking my business chores in order to visit with a client. I've learned that money can buy a lot of useful things (like health insurance!), but not love or good health.

So it wasn't hard to make a break with the drive of the corporate world and start a business venture with my sister. Still, the first day we opened for business, I remember feeling my stomach sink as minutes passed by and no one came. But slowly, one by one, women walked in the door and signed on as members.

Five years have passed since our grand opening, and we're still going strong. Our membership ranges from a young teen to several ladies in their eighties. At any given moment, we see fortyish stay-at-home moms working out next to thirtysomething lawyers and teachers. Talk about enlightening conversations—a group of women representing a wide spectrum of lifestyles and experiences contributing to one another and cheering each other on.

Each lady comes for a different reason and stays for the same reason: the friendships they make here. We're a family—we gather together to share with one another and to feel better about ourselves physically and mentally. Our members' buddy referrals are our greatest asset to our growth—and a testimony to their confidence in us, the two sisters.

I know we're a big part of the success story, too. Our members talk about "the other sister" when one of us is missing. They play tricks on us, provoking us to difficult "sister moments," and chuckle at the responses we trade with one another. She and I are as different as can be, she the organized, creative worrier and I the story-telling, live-in-the-moment jokester, which sometimes translates into tension. Most of the time, our head-butting sessions are comical and contribute to the family-like atmosphere at our facility.

> My sister and I opened a small business with the hope of creating a better life for ourselves. Little did we know that we would create a better life for many others.

Our mother has even jumped on the bandwagon and started exercising at our center. She will celebrate her eighty-fourth birthday this year and consistently exercises three times each week. Most of our members know our mother—and most even call her Mom.

When I asked one of our other older members why she exercises with us, she replied, "What good is it if I keep my mind in shape and my body falls apart?"

Just the other day, one of our members said, "I hope you both realize what you did by opening this place here. You gave us a spot to come and de-stress. You created a place where we feel we can come and be ourselves but not be by ourselves."

My sister and I started our own business with the hope of creating a better life for ourselves. Little did we know that we would create a better life for many others. I may have less in my wallet, but I certainly have more in my life. I like it that way. Even if I have to pay for my own medical benefits, it was worth starting a new adventure alongside my sister and lots of caring women I would have never met otherwise. ⬡

I AM THE LORD YOUR GOD,
WHO HOLDS YOUR RIGHT HAND,
AND I TELL YOU, "DON'T
BE AFRAID. I WILL HELP YOU."

ISAIAH 41:13

They Said It

The future is always beginning now.

MARK STRAND

When you are through changing, you are through.

BRUCE BARTON

We all have big changes in our lives
that are more or less a second chance.

HARRISON FORD

Remember today, for it is the beginning of always. Today marks
the start of a brave new future filled with all your dreams can hold.
Think truly to the future and make those dreams come true.

ANONYMOUS

Being stuck is a position few of us like. We want something new but
cannot let go of the old—old ideas, beliefs, habits, even thoughts.
We are out of contact with our own genius. Sometimes we know we are
stuck; sometimes we don't. In both cases we have to do something.

RUSH LIMBAUGH

Nobody can go back and start a new beginning,
but anyone can start today and make a new ending.

MARIA ROBINSON

With God's power working in us, God can do much, much more than anything we can ask or imagine.

EPHESIANS 3:20

Where Is Your Calcutta?

CHRISTY PHILLIPPE

Mother Teresa has inspired millions of people with her life of sacrificial service. One such woman was so affected by her life and calling that she decided to give up her privileged life in the United States, move to Calcutta, and share in Mother Teresa's ministry.

When Mother Teresa heard of the woman's plans, she did not respond with the expected enthusiasm. Instead, she wrote the woman this brief, yet profound, reply: "Find your own Calcutta."

Where is your Calcutta? Perhaps it's right in your own back yard. ⬡

A History of Hair

Our hair has been used to make a statement for millennia—archaeologists have found primitive boxwood combs among the oldest of artifacts. You can't count on hair trends to stay the same for longer than about a month, but some things never change.

- The ponytail. A longtime favorite on rushed mornings, the ponytail first appeared on ancient Greek frescoes and has survived and thrived into the twenty-first century. Whether piled high "I Dream of Jeannie" style or tightly banded for a sleek, Audrey-Hepburn-at-the-prom look, women will always love a ponytail.

- Braids. Braids became fashionable for women in the Middle Ages, and twentieth-century moms knew them well as a quick, durable hairstyle for their little girls. Dreadlock-style braids and cornrows made a lasting resurgence in the 1960s, while the early 90s enjoyed a few years of French braid bliss. We're told French braids are about to become "edgy"; we're not sure about that, since we remember our aunts French braiding our hair immediately before taking us horseback riding. In any case, we're sure that braids in some form will always be with us.

- Color. Wealthy Romans sometimes sprinkled gold dust in their hair to achieve the coveted blond mane. During the Renaissance, painter Titian popularized strawberry-blond hair for women, prompting Venetian women to paste their hair with a mixture of alum, sulfur, and soda in an attempt to dye it, and we all remember pastel powdered wigs from our history textbooks. Today, with the variety and availability of permanent hair color, color or highlights are a given for many women—the only question is which color.

- Clip and Curl. The twentieth century, with its increasingly rapid communication media, has seen more changes in hairstyle than ever before. To the horror of many, the short bob was popularized in the 1920s, and since then, our hair length has vacillated between long and short—from the superlong hippie braid to the Vidal Sassoon bob to Mia Farrow's close crop. Likewise, we've wandered among finger waves, tight spiral perms, and chic, string-straight styles. If you're wistful for the hairstyles of your youth, just wait a few years—they'll come back.

Throughout history, we've used our hair to tell the world where we've been and where we're going—that we're cultured or idealistic or modern. Usually we want our hairstyle to be easy; but always we want our hair to be beautiful. ⬡

Hair brings one's self-image into focus;
it is vanity's proving ground.
Hair is terribly personal, a tangle
of mysterious prejudices.

SHANA ALEXANDER

Gray hair is like a crown of honor; it is earned by living a good life.

PROVERBS 16:31

The Advantages of Age

BETTY JO MINGS

Old age has some advantages (or so I have been told.)
They help to dull the trauma that occurs when growing old.

I don my purple dress and slip into supportive shoes,
And kind friends always help me find the articles I lose.

When sermons are so boring that my eyelids start to fold,
I know I'll be forgiven just because I'm growing old.

I hug a handsome man who has a problem or a hurt.
His wife is never jealous, nor suspects that I'm a flirt.

When asked a simple question, and my answer seems obtuse,
I never need to worry, for old age is my excuse.

I learn a lot of information as I linger near,
For people blab some juicy secrets, thinking I can't hear.

There's lots of kind assistance as I hobble on my way,
And my age is my alibi for silly things I say.

Yes, age has its advantages, and though it's sometimes rough,
It slowly comes to all of us if we live long enough.

Yet age is not for sissies, and it takes strength to endure.
But I will thrive while I'm alive, for death's the only cure. ⬡

*God speaks to us through
our desires, then as we
lay them at His feet,
He helps us sort them
out and quiets our hearts
to accept what He
has already prepared.*

ROSALIND RINKER

The Classics

CAROL GENENGELS

As a mother, I've learned that having grown sons often demands long-suffering. Their toys aren't as easy to pick up and put away as their matchbox cars were. Take Ryan's motorcycle, for instance. Though he hadn't ridden it in years, the bike held a place of honor in the blackberry bushes. "I'm gonna restore it someday, Mom—I can't get rid of it!" My youngest child, Ryan knew he could usually wrap me around his little finger. As a teen, he once accused me of child abuse for buying fat-free ice cream.

When he drove off to college in a pickup, he abandoned his first love, a black '77 Camaro, next to his brother's red '67 Firebird and '79 Datsun with no windows. Next to the cars, a sixteen-foot boat and trailer languished in the sun.

Ryan, home for summer break, was busy working in the back yard when I approached him. He was tenderly spreading gobs of Bondo over the rust spots of his Camaro. "Listen, Ryan," I said lightly, "since you drive that truck now, why not sell the Camaro?"

"Sell the Camaro!" Ryan gasped as if I'd asked him to cut off his foot. His expression of sheer terror let me know I'd have to tread carefully. He continued, "When I get it all fixed, it'll be worth a lot more than I paid for it. It'll be a classic someday!"

"I can hardly wait," I muttered before returning to the house to consider my next tactics.

Number one son, Shawn, the owner of the Firebird and Datsun, came over to work on a marine engine. I found him under the sun deck, muscles rippling as he hoisted an outboard motor into a barrel of fresh water. I sauntered over and plied gently: "Say, Shawn, have you considered selling that Firebird? You never drive it anymore."

Ryan gasped as if I'd asked him to cut off his foot. His expression of sheer terror let me know I'd have to tread carefully. "When I get it all fixed, it'll be worth a lot more than I paid for it. It'll be a classic someday!"

Shawn wiped grimy hands on his jeans. His blue eyes stared as though I'd said something ridiculous. "Mom, that car has sentimental value. I bought that in the Navy, remember? It took me ages to pay it off. Besides it's almost a classic!"

"Well, what about the Datsun?" I persisted.

"Aw, Mom, nobody will buy that thing the way it is. New windows will cost more than it's worth. I'll probably have it hauled away."

I sighed and went back into the house. I recalled the day Shawn parked his Datsun at the top of the road with a "For Sale" sign. In the middle of the night vandals broke out all of the windows. The next day Shawn sadly brought it down the hill and parked it next to his Firebird.

My husband, Ted, came up from the basement. "Carol, have you seen my torque wrench?"

"I wouldn't know a torque wrench if I stumbled over one. Try the back yard."

"Those guys never put anything away," he mumbled.

"Ted, our back yard looks like a junkyard!" I said, seizing the opportunity to complain.

"What's wrong with it?"

"It's all those cars! Shawn's Firebird, the Datsun, that boat and trailer nobody uses, and Ryan's Camaro and truck."

"There's nothing wrong with Ryan's truck."

"That's not the point! With our cars and all their junkers, our house looks like a used car lot in a bad part of town! This is a nice neighborhood, or at least it was!"

"I would like to get rid of that Datsun," Ted admitted. "It's a shame about those windows."

As summer progressed, I grew to hate those cars. As much as I prayed that the Lord would spur my boys to car-selling action—or maybe just consume the cars in a freak fireball—I also prayed for my own attitude. *Lord, help me be patient and understanding.*

Everyone who entered our yard was asked the same question: "Do you know anyone who needs an old Datsun with no windows?" No one jumped at my offer.

By spring the tarps had blown off, and mushrooms were sprouting in the back seat. Please, Lord, send someone to take this wreck away.

One day, I got tough. "Shawn, it's almost wintertime—you'd better do something about that Datsun, and soon!"

"Okay, Mom, I promise I'll take care of it tomorrow."

When I came home from work the next day, the Datsun was draped with blue tarps. "Aughhhhhhhh!"

By spring the tarps had blown off, and mushrooms were sprouting in the back seat. *Please, Lord, send someone to take this wreck away.*

Meanwhile, Ted was asked to consider running for president of the small mission congregation we attended. He took the matter to the Lord in prayer, but heard nothing. Pastor Tim called at the beginning of the week saying he needed an answer by the following Sunday. All week Ted wrestled with his decision.

"You'd better let Pastor Tim know pretty soon," I said. It was Saturday afternoon, and he still had no answer.

He shook his head. "I just don't know."

"Hey, why don't we put out a fleece?" I suggested.

Ted frowned, "What kind of a fleece?"

"Well, you know—something so out of the ordinary that if it happens, you'll know for sure that you're supposed to serve as president. I've got an idea. Let's tell God that if somebody walks down our driveway tonight and buys that old Datsun, then you'll know."

Ted laughed, "I guess we're safe on that one."

"I'm serious! Let's pray."

About 9:30 that evening, Ted said, "I'd better call the pastor. I hate to let him down, but—"

Just then, the doorbell rang. Our teenage neighbor, Alex, and a friend of his greeted us. "Hi, Mrs. Genengels," he nodded politely, "Mr. Genengels."

"Hi, Alex, what's up?"

"Well, my friend was wondering if you'd take fifty bucks for that Datsun." We doubled over.

"What's so funny?" Alex asked.

"Are you sure you want that car?"

His friend answered, "Yeah, it's perfect for demolition derby. I've had my eye on it for awhile."

"You've got yourself a deal!" Ted said before excusing himself. "I have to call someone."

Ted served as congregational president for two years. Remarkably, all the "classics" eventually found new back yards to rest in. And I have discovered that while being the mother of grown sons has its own special challenges, it certainly comes in handy when one needs something completely out of the ordinary. ⬡

I AM THE LORD YOUR GOD, WHO TEACHES YOU TO DO WHAT
IS GOOD, WHO LEADS YOU IN THE WAY YOU SHOULD GO.

ISAIAH 48:17

The Road Not Taken

ROBERT FROST

Two roads diverged in a yellow wood,
And sorry I could not travel both
And be one traveler, long I stood
And looked down one as far as I could
To where it bent in the undergrowth.

Then took the other, as just as fair,
And having perhaps the better claim,
Because it was grassy and wanted wear;
Though as for that the passing there
Had worn them really about the same,

And both that morning equally lay
In leaves no step had trodden black.
Oh, I kept the first for another day!
Yet knowing how way leads on to way,
I doubted if I should ever come back.

I shall be telling this with a sigh
Somewhere ages and ages hence:
Two roads diverged in a wood, and I—
I took the one less traveled by,
And that has made all the difference.

Change Is Good

Are you ready for a brand-new you? Are you craving change? Maybe you should think about making a change to your hair. This is obviously something to consider carefully—platinum blonde is not for everyone. Do a little research and ask friends for advice to pick something out that maximizes your natural beauty and reflects your personality. A few helpful hints include—

- Work with your face shape. If you have an oval face, avoid heavy bangs or forward-sweeping styles that cover you up. If your face is long and rectangular, look for short to medium cuts with fullness at the sides to add balance. Round faces look great with styles longer than chin length and off-center parts, as do heart-shaped faces.

- Prepare your family. For their heart health, make sure they know what you're planning!

- Sleep on it. Don't make an appointment until you've had a chance to think it over. You might even want to talk to more than one stylist, taking along some pictures to get some advice and get a feel for their work.

And if it doesn't quite work, don't worry—even if it's not immediately fixable, it will eventually grow back, and you can take comfort in knowing that you're the dynamic, risk-taking type. When it comes to hair, at least. ⬢

Joke Break

Never underestimate the power of a bad joke. These groaners might just inspire you to do something brand-new, if for no other reason than to do something besides read jokes!

How did the boo-tician style the ghost's hair?
With a scare dryer.

What do cows wear when they're vacationing in Hawaii?
Moo-moos.

What dreams does a plumber have?
Pipe dreams.

A Brand-New Day

GENESIS 12:1-9

Every one of us wants to live a happy life—a blessed life. But the story of Abraham reminds us that experiencing this kind of life doesn't come from focusing on our own needs, but rather from two very simple—and sometimes difficult—decisions on our part.

The first decision is trust: "I'll obey God, no matter what." God called Abraham to leave his familiar homeland, where he was prosperous and comfortable, to do something great for Him. This meant a great journey to an unknown land and living in nomadic tents rather than permanent palaces.

Does that mean obedience will always be unpleasant? Jesus reminds us that His "yoke is easy" (Matthew 11:30) and that when we make the fundamental decision to obey, our lives will be blessed beyond measure.

The second decision is to bless others. Abraham was blessed in order to be a blessing. Perhaps there is no greater source of unhappiness than when we live only for ourselves.

When did King David get into trouble? When he stayed behind in comfort rather than journey out to serve his troops. Paul's love for the "baby churches" he helped to start was so great that he said, "Yes, and if I am being poured out as a drink offering on the sacrifice and service of your faith, I am glad and rejoice with you all" (Philippians 2:17 NKJV). He literally gave his life for others, in the same way Jesus did. No truly great endeavor can ever be self-focused.

What's around the corner in your life? An exciting new day is yours as you step out in obedience and service to others. ⬡

> HE GIVES ME NEW STRENGTH.
> HE LEADS ME ON PATHS THAT ARE RIGHT
> FOR THE GOOD OF HIS NAME.
>
> **PSALM 23:3**

God's Promises
for New Beginnings

God will...

Show you what to do

If you go the wrong way—to the right or to the left—
you will hear a voice behind you saying,
"This is the right way. You should go this way."

ISAIAH 30:21

Be with you

Even if I walk through a very dark valley,
I will not be afraid, because you are with me.

PSALM 23:4

Give you what you need

Jesus has the power of God, by which he has given
us everything we need to live and to serve God.

2 PETER 1:3

Unburden you
Come to me, all of you who are tired and
have heavy loads, and I will give you rest.

MATTHEW 11:28

Help you when you're tired
My body and my mind may become weak,
but God is my strength.

PSALM 73:26

Continue to work in your life
God began doing a good work in you, and
I am sure he will continue it until it is
finished when Jesus Christ comes again.

PHILIPPIANS 1:6

Give you more as you are faithful with what you have
Because you were loyal with small things,
I will let you care for much greater things.
Come and share my joy with me.

MATTHEW 25:21

A Prayer of Joy and Thanksgiving

Dear Heavenly Father,

*You know the times when I strayed onto paths
that You didn't want me to take. I am sorry for
my carelessness and my stubbornness, for those
times when I just didn't have the faith to believe
that You know what's best for me—every time.
I do acknowledge that You alone are completely
trustworthy. And so it is with confidence and
gratitude that I commit all the areas of my life to You.
Show me Your will and guide my steps today.*

*Thank You, God, for guiding me back onto the right
paths for my life through Your patience and love.*

HIGHLIGHTS AND COLOR

There is no beautifier of complexion, or form, or behavior, like the wish to scatter joy and not pain around us.

RALPH WALDO EMERSON

I know God wants me to be humble, but I have to admit, sometimes it's fun to sparkle and glow. I was raised that it's not right to draw attention to myself. And I know that true beauty is a matter of the heart. But when I got home from hair appointment and my seventeen-year-old said, "Wow," it absolutely made my day, week, and month.

"Garden Party" and "Mowing Over the Gifts" are great reminders that life is to be lived joyfully!

THE LORD TAKES PLEASURE IN THOSE WHO FEAR HIM,
IN THOSE WHO HOPE IN HIS MERCY.

PSALM 147:11 NKJV

*I've never seen
a smiling face
that was not
beautiful.*

AUTHOR UNKNOWN

Garden Party

CHARLENE FRIESEN

While leaning on my shovel one hot afternoon, I surveyed my landscaping project and made a mental list: Grass planted? Check. Peat moss mixed with soil? Check. Rock border in place? Check. Major shrubs planted? Check.

Still, something wasn't quite right. The dirt was too clean and tidy, the plants looked too regimented. I needed a few rambunctious plants to kick up their heels and loosen up my sensible and solemn garden. Unfortunately, I had just pruned my money tree, so a trip to the nursery was not an option. I drove to the next best source for plants: my parent's garden.

Armed with my spade and a box, I spied some alyssum and a blue weed-like plant. "What's this?" I asked my dad, pointing to the weedy specimen with my muddy shoe. "Those are called forget-me-nots," he said. "It's a self-seeding plant and a super rockery filler." Sold! I grabbed my shovel and eagerly dug up about twenty tiny, tender plants.

Once at home, I went right to work baptizing my new little flower friends with dirt and water. I dubbed the forget-me-not flowers "my ladies" and indulged them like a grandma who has nothing but time and chocolate bars for her grandchildren. I lavishly gave them attention, encouragement, and healthy applications of fertilizer.

Soon, my ladies perked up. They threw their shoulders back and in time were saluting me with their delicate blue flowers. I enjoyed watching them spread their arms and twirl in the breeze. Their dance even spilled onto the rockery border, giving my strait-laced garden a whimsical touch.

As winter approached, I wondered how my ladies would cope. I anxiously peered through my window and hoped they were keeping warm in the chilly wind and rain.

Soon, my ladies were perking up. They threw their shoulders back and in time were saluting me with their delicate blue flowers. I enjoyed watching them spread their arms and twirl in the breeze. Their dance even spilled onto the rockery border, giving my strait-laced garden a whimsical touch.

In time, the sun nudged the winter rain aside, and I wandered through my garden once again. My crocuses winked and nodded their colorful, smiling faces. Spring was open for business.

I stooped over my garden and nosily poked around in the soil. The ladies in blue were back with a vengeance. Not only had they survived the winter, they were flourishing in the spring. It looked like my forget-me-nots had hosted a Christmas party and their guests had never left.

In time, my sculpted, uptight garden developed a cheeky attitude. The shrubs relaxed and kicked off their shoes. Through the spring and summer, the forget-me-nots tirelessly filled my garden with vibrancy, just a little bit of chaos, and a style all their own.

I want to be remembered as one who had a distinctive, memorable style. I have taken to wearing leopard-print velvet shoes, for example, and I have already placed my order for a big bunch of forget-me-nots to be planted on my grave. Hopefully, family and friends will chuckle and remember the resilient little lady who willingly ventured onto the rocky, less traveled path, seeding the love and hope of Jesus.

Until that time, I will continue to give friends and family a tour of my garden and ample cuttings of forget-me-nots. "Here," I say, as I stand amidst patches of color, delightfully dirty soil, and endearing disorder, "let me give you something to remember me by."

GOOD PEOPLE WILL ALWAYS BE REMEMBERED.

PSALM 112:6

They Said It

I'm not offended by all the dumb-blonde jokes because
I know that I'm not dumb. I also know I'm not blonde.

DOLLY PARTON

What we are is God's gift to us. What we become is our gift to God.

ELEANOR POWELL

Whether you think you can or think you can't—you are right.

HENRY FORD

Rabbi Zusya said that on the Day of Judgment, God would ask him,
not why he had not been Moses, but why he had not been Zusya.

WALTER KAUFMANN

*Now wherever we go he uses us to tell
others about the Lord and to spread the
Good News like a sweet perfume.*

2 CORINTHIANS 2:14 NLT

The Fragrance of Friendship

CHRISTY PHILLIPPE

Mary is one of my best—and most unique—friends. She loves collecting and wearing a breathtaking—literally—array of perfumes. Many of her friends and relatives, familiar with Mary's predilection for fragrances, love to buy her new perfumes as gifts.

Mary is also a cheerful and loving person who enjoys hugging other people—friend or stranger! When Mary gives me a hug, her fragrance rubs off on me, and I remember her warmth and friendship for hours because the scent of her perfume lingers on my clothing.

When I think of Mary, I think of her cheerfulness and the sweet-smelling friendship she brings. I hope that my friendship, too, "rubs off" on others and is a fragrance that brings a smile to their face when they think of me. ⬢

*Love is a game
that two can play
and both win.*

EVA GABOR

Schemers Never Prosper

NANCY C. ANDERSON

I squealed with joy as happy tears splashed on my go-go boots. The Beatles were on the Ed Sullivan show and I watched with enraptured bliss. I knew that I was in love with Paul McCartney. I knew that somehow, some way, he would find me and marry me. I was a fourth-grader and an optimist.

While I waited for Paul to come searching for me in Winona, Minnesota, I found a stand-in. Jack was the cutest boy in our class, and the day he came to school with a Beatle haircut, I was captivated. I had never spoken to Jack because he was one of the cool kids. I was only average, in every way except one: I was an excellent schemer.

One morning, Jack got in trouble for passing a note to Wendy (another cool kid—she owned a horse) and the teacher sentenced him to after-school detention. That meant he would have to clean all the chalkboard erasers in the entire school. *Ah-ha, I thought, here's my chance.* I was relentlessly obnoxious for the rest of the day until I earned my detention.

Jack and I went from room to room, asking the teachers for their blackboard erasers. Then we took them into the janitor's closet, where we fed them into a cleaning machine. With each grinding, swishing sound, with each breath of chalk dust, I fell deeper in love. When his hand brushed against mine, goose bumps scurried up my arm. He started to talk to me as if I was cool, and suddenly, I was. The next day, he gave me a note containing the deepest, most meaningful words I had ever read: "I like you." Our romance lasted for several months, until I outgrew him and developed a killer crush on a sixth grader who looked like Davy Jones of the Monkees.

Here's my chance, I thought. I was relentlessly obnoxious for the rest of the day until I earned my detention.

The summer between sixth and seventh grade, I gave my first kiss to my neighbor Billy. Well...actually, he bought it from me.

I was working outside, pulling weeds in my front yard when Billy careened around the corner on his red Stingray bike. He skidded to a stop in front of me and said, "I got you somethin'." He held up a little stuffed animal—a mouse.

Billy said, "I heard you tell my sister that you wanted this, that you'd do just about anything to get it, so I bought it from her. I'll give it to ya— for a kiss." Without a hint of hesitation, I leaned over the bike, kissed him full on the lips, grabbed the mouse, and ran. We both got what we wanted—fair trade. My scheming was paying off.

My next little caper didn't go as well. By the time I got to high school, I was crazy in love with Jimmy. I wrote him poem after poem. He said that I was a great writer and, of course, I believed him. But secretly, I wondered if I could keep writing such epic poetry. One day, as I was sitting on my bed, trying to think of a non-offensive rhyme for *heart*, I heard a breathtaking song on an old Peter, Paul, and Mary album. The lyrics were haunting. My devious mind kicked into high gear and developed a plan—*he'll never know that I didn't write it. He would never listen to an album by folk singers. He's a rock n' roll guy—I can get away with it.* I wrote down the first verse to the song, and signed my name to it.

Jimmy was amazed at my new creation. He said, "I think you could sell this. Seriously, it's really, really good!" I explained, "You were my inspiration; it just says how I feel about you—about us."

A week later, I was riding in the car with my mother when a DJ announced the title of a new hit single. I froze. That was the name of "my" poem! The deep, rich voice of Roberta Flack sang, "The first time ever I saw your face—I thought the sun rose in your eyes...." Jimmy never spoke to me again.

> I was riding in the car with my mother when a DJ announced the title of a new hit single. I froze. That was the name of the poem I'd copied!

My scheming was beginning to backfire.

However, I didn't fully learn my lesson until several years later, after I married Ron, my college sweetheart. Even though I had become a Christian, I was still selfish and manipulative: I was a terrible wife. It was only after I almost lost my marriage that I realized that the road to love is not a one-way street.

I asked the Lord to help me to put His love into action. I began to live the verse in 1 Corinthians 13, "Love is not rude, is not selfish, and does not get upset with others." I learned to find joy in serving others and looked for ways to help my husband accomplish his goals. He, in turn, has helped me accomplish mine. We are now walking down Lovers Lane as a team, holding hands, side-by-side.

Next year we will celebrate our twenty-eighth anniversary and the only thing I'm scheming about is how to surprise him with a trip to Hawaii. ⬡

LOVE IS PATIENT AND KIND. LOVE IS NOT JEALOUS,
IT DOES NOT BRAG, AND IT IS NOT PROUD.

1 CORINTHIANS 13:4

Advice to Myself

1. Read e-mails before sending them.
2. Don't eat anything for breakfast that would be too rich as a dessert.
3. Don't buy anything just because it's on sale.
4. Four-inch stilettos are for runway models and podiatry patients.
5. Make sure you get or give five hugs a day.
6. Don't spend more than thirty seconds a day regretting the past.
7. Don't spend more than thirty seconds a day worrying about the future.
8. Call your siblings once a week, your parents twice.
9. Listen well.
10. Rent a foreign movie every now and then.
11. Don't straighten your hair if it wants to be curly.
12. Eat your vegetables.
13. Listen to your mother.
14. Don't dwell on hurtful words.
15. Make an effort to say helpful words.
16. Don't drive faster than you want your kids to drive.
17. Watch less than a sitcom's worth of TV a day.
18. Set goals.
19. Spend less on coffee than you do on groceries.
20. Write out your grandparents' life stories.
21. Read a book a week.
22. Organize your bills.
23. Apologize quickly.
24. Don't procrastinate.

25. Remember names.

26. Be nice to yourself—you may be the only one to be nice to you all day.

27. Eat a favorite food once a week.

28. Find a friend to exercise with.

29. Be a kid every now and then—swing on swing sets, giggle at cartoons, or drink chocolate milk.

30. Learn to say no.

31. Drink eight glasses of water a day.

32. Pick out a new recipe and serve a fun dinner every now and then.

33. Fill the ice trays as soon as they're empty.

34. Learn a new hobby.

35. Make banana bread when bananas get too ripe to eat plain.

36. Get your oil changed when you should.

37. Meet two new people a week.

38. Work hard.

39. Don't work too hard.

40. Be nice to animals.

41. Ask questions.

42. Don't beat yourself up for not cleaning the baseboards.

43. Clean the baseboards.

44. Get a pedicure or a foot massage when you need to de-stress.

45. Take walks.

46. Stock your car console with mints, maps, and change.

47. Make copies of everything in your wallet in case it gets stolen.

48. Keep insurance and credit card phone numbers in a safe, yet easily accessible place.

49. Drink green tea.

50. Have fun.

You Are Special

One of the deepest and most meaningful ways to sparkle and glow is to revel in the great love of God, a love we find throughout Scripture—

- "The Father has loved us so much that we are called children of God. And we really are his children" (1 John 3:1).

- "I love you people with a love that will last forever. That is why I have continued showing you kindness" (Jeremiah 31:3).

- "God loved us, and through his grace he gave us a good hope and encouragement that continues forever" (2 Thessalonians 2:17).

- "But God shows his great love for us in this way: Christ died for us while we were still sinners" (Romans 5:8).

To fill your day with God's love, write these verses out on notecards and tape them on the mirrors in your house so that every time you and your family see yourselves, you know how loved you are. ⬡

*You were born
an original.
Don't die a copy.*

JOHN MASON

Hair Fact and Fiction

We'll do just about anything to keep our hair beautiful, as evidenced by how many of us fall victim to hair care myths—

- *Rinse an egg white in your hair for optimum hair health.* The protein in the egg white might soothe your hair a little, but most experts agree that vitamins, proteins, and amino acids do the most good for your hair when eaten in healthy food, not applied topically. Besides, who likes semi-cooked egg white in their shower drain?

- *Frequent haircuts make hair grow faster.* Given a few dietary and hormonal provisos, hair more or less grows as fast as it wants to.

- *Brush your hair 100 strokes a day.* No offense to Marcia Brady, but overbrushing can pull hairs out of their follicles and possibly damage hair.

- *Rinsing with cold water will make your hair shinier and smoother.* While there is some debate about the benefits of cool water versus hot, *Good Housekeeping* contends that cold water does nothing to shine and smooth your hair.

The best thing about your hair is its natural beauty. So don't stress or worry about making your hair beautiful—just keep it healthy and it will glow on its own. ⬡

Joke Break

If there's nothing more beautiful than a smile, we're not sure these jokes will do much for you—eye-rolling is probably a much lesser beautifier than smiling. But on the plus side, if you tell these jokes to your kindergartener, he'll probably think you're funny.

Why do bees have sticky hair?
They use honeycombs.

Where do sheep get a haircut?
At the baa-baa shop.

Man in uniform: "Catch any fish this morning?"
Fisherman: "Yep—caught over thirty fish."
Man in uniform: "Do you know who I am? I'm the game warden, and
you've caught way over your legal limit."
Fisherman: "Do you know who I am?
I'm the biggest liar on the lake."

*Always be a first-rate
version of yourself,
instead of a second-rate
version of somebody else.*

JUDY GARLAND

Mowing Over the Gifts

MIGNON MURRELL

Ah, spring is in the air, and you know what that means: yard work, two of the most dreaded words in my language. I hate yard work. Even as a child, my voice frequently rang out: "I'll eat the spinach and Brussels sprouts, just please don't make me rake the leaves!" I thought buying a house with a beautiful yard full of trees would encourage me to have a change of heart, but I was wrong.

Because I am usually the only one home during the day, the job of mowing and raking the yard often falls to me. This requires that I become familiar with yard accessories known as "tools." Mind you, the tools belong to my husband, Bill; he just loans them to me for special projects like cutting and raking his yard. Even though I get to use these precious tools, I don't necessarily always know how to operate them correctly.

I took the scissors out to attack the lawn. As I knelt down and started to snip away at the long blades of grass, my husband drove up. He rolled down his window and, with a bemused look on his face, had the nerve to say, "Uh, honey, things might go a little faster if you used the lawnmower."

For example, recently I was mowing the lawn when I noticed a section of the grass that I couldn't cut. Every time I mowed over it, the grass would lie down as if playing possum. Now, being a lazy perfectionist (and yes, that is a real title—I made it up myself), I was determined to cut the stubborn area. I ran over it seventeen more times before I finally decided to bring out the big guns: I went in and got the scissors.

Ah, scissors—one of the greatest tools ever invented. They are so useful for more than just cutting things. For instance, I use them to pull nails out of the walls when I am hanging pictures. This keeps me from having to call Bill and ask him where the tool that pulls nails out of the wall might actually be in our garage. When Bill goes to use our scissors, he sees that they are bent and asks me what happened. I shrug with a look of innocence and promptly change the subject.

As I was saying, I took the scissors out to attack the lawn. As I knelt down and started to snip away at the long blades of grass, my husband drove up. He rolled down his window and, with a bemused look on his face, had the nerve to say, "Uh, honey, things might go a little faster if you used the lawnmower."

"Gee," I replied with a healthy dose of sarcasm, "What a great idea! Why didn't I think of that?"

When Bill finally thought it was safe to step out of the truck, he went over to the lawnmower and announced that he had found the reason for my problem. The mower's wheels were set too high and needed to be adjusted. I only thought I had been cutting the yard—in reality I had only been taking a little off the top and the sides. To Bill's credit, he didn't mock my lack of Lawnmower 101 skills; he simply reset the wheels and went inside the house to finish laughing hysterically.

God gives each of us a set of tools that we are to use—gifts. But many times, like me and my lawnmower, we use them without really knowing how to operate them correctly. The gift of encouragement or intercession for someone who has asked for prayers in confidence becomes an opportunity to mow the person down in gossip. Or the chance to share the gift of wisdom and discernment with a friend becomes an opportunity to nail them with judgment. The gift of mercy or service can be snipped away by the scissors of resentment and a constant desire to be acknowledged.

Likewise, we use our gifts most effectively when, instead of envying the gifts of others, we embrace ourselves and our gifts and ask God to use us as He sees fit.

Learning to use our gifts correctly lightens our load and makes our journey here much easier—unlike the lawn that I had to re-mow. Make no mistake, next spring I'll be sure the mower is set correctly before I start in on the lawn. Who knows—I might even start to like yard work by then. ⬢

WE ALL HAVE DIFFERENT GIFTS,
EACH OF WHICH CAME BECAUSE
OF THE GRACE GOD GAVE US.

ROMANS 12:6

Shining Like a Star

PHILIPPIANS 2:15

You've heard all the advice on how to get noticed, how to stand out. It usually involves tips on clothes and makeup and hairstyle and how to give a good handshake. But the Apostle Paul had some other ideas on how to stand out.

Paul wrote two letters to his young protégé, Timothy, giving special attention to Timothy's integrity. He wanted him to exhibit a blameless, godly lifestyle of purity through his words and actions.

Paul's biggest concern for this young pastor and the young church was expressed when he said: "But if I am delayed, I write so that you may know how you ought to conduct yourself in the house of God, which is the church of the living God, the pillar and ground of the truth" (1 Timothy 3:15 NKJV). As the Christian Church grew and made headway in an immoral (or amoral) and permissive culture, there were a myriad of questions raised by new believers about ethics and truth.

Though Paul recognized that there can be legitimate disagreements on matters of conscience, one non-negotiable was that followers of Jesus Christ should have the highest standard of honesty.

Even in the church in Jerusalem, where it was expected that members came from a more honest and moral society, lying was a problem and was judged with severity. (See the story of Ananias and Sapphira in Acts 5.)

We, too, live in a permissive society that does not always show high regard for honesty and integrity, for doing the right thing. We have the same opportunity as Timothy and the early Christian church to make a profound impact on others through the way we conduct our lives. Paul expressed this prayer for another first-century church: "that you may become blameless and harmless, children of God without fault in the midst of a crooked and perverse generation, among whom you shine as lights in the world" (Philippians 2:15 NKJV). ⬡

> ALSO TODAY THE LORD HAS PROCLAIMED
> YOU TO BE HIS SPECIAL PEOPLE, JUST
> AS HE PROMISED YOU, THAT YOU
> SHOULD KEEP ALL HIS COMMANDMENTS.
>
> **DEUTERONOMY 26:18 NKJV**

God's Promises for Self-Acceptance

God will...

Honor your inner beauty

No, your beauty should come from within you—
the beauty of a gentle and quiet spirit that will never
be destroyed and is very precious to God.

1 PETER 3:4

Judge you by your faith, not your level of perfection

So we, too, have put our faith in Christ Jesus, that we might
be made right with God because we trusted in Christ.

GALATIANS 2:16

Delight in you

He does not enjoy the strength of a horse or
the strength of a man. The Lord is pleased with those
who respect him, with those who trust his love.

PSALM 147:10–11

Bear fruit in your life

I am the vine, and you are the branches. If any
remain in me and I remain in them, they produce
much fruit. But without me they can do nothing.

JOHN 15:5

Cause you to flourish

The Lord will always lead you. He will satisfy your needs in dry lands and give strength to your bones. You will be like a garden that has much water, like a spring that never runs dry.

ISAIAH 58:11

Perfect your character

But let patience have its perfect work, that you may be perfect and complete, lacking nothing.

JAMES 1:4 NKJV

Cause you to shine

You will be God's children without fault. But you are living with crooked and mean people all around you, among whom you shine like stars in the dark world.

PHILIPPIANS 2:15

Use you

But thanks be to God, who always leads us in victory through Christ. God uses us to spread his knowledge everywhere like a sweet-smelling perfume.

2 CORINTHIANS 2:14

A Prayer of Praise and Thanksgiving

Dear Heavenly Father,

*Thank You, Lord, that You delight in me.
I'm so honored that You call me Your child, and
that You're such a great Daddy to me. Thank You
for Your blessings. Thank You for making my life
challenging and fun. Thank You for helping me
grow in You and as a person.*

*Help me enjoy the gifts You've given me
and use them to bless others.*

A LITTLE HELP, PLEASE

A woman under stress is not immediately concerned with finding solutions to her problems but rather seeks relief by expressing herself and being understood.

JOHN GRAY

The problem isn't just my hair. Company gets here in less than an hour and the potatoes aren't in the oven, the roast is severely overcooked, I broke my only good serving platter, and the kids haven't run the vacuum cleaner or swept leaves off the front porch like I asked.

We really do need help sometimes. Just ask Nanette Thorsen-Snipes after reading the story "A Thankful Heart." The good news is God is always the Friend we need.

IN THE MULTITUDE OF MY ANXIETIES WITHIN ME,
YOUR COMFORTS DELIGHT MY SOUL.

PSALM 94:19 NKJV

Are you upset, little friend?
Have you been lying awake worrying?
Well, don't worry—I'm here.
The flood waters will recede,
the famine will end, the sun will
shine tomorrow, and I will
always be here to take care of you.

CHARLES SCHULTZ'S CHARLIE BROWN TO SNOOPY

A Thankful Heart

NANETTE THORSEN-SNIPES

The day was supposed to be a day set aside for gratitude—Thanksgiving. But this cool November day, the wind whistling outside, I was less than thankful. I fished another boiled egg from the pot, and as I began shelling, I could feel the angry heat rush to my cheeks. My husband had helped me start the turkey, then squirreled himself away on the sofa.

"Do you need any help?" he asked as he peered from behind the sports page.

"No," I answered tersely. I tossed the half-peeled egg into the pan. I could feel the tears building and I fought the feelings of self-pity beginning inside me. I picked up the hospital bracelet my daughter had just taken off and shot it into the trash.

Just two days earlier, I had rushed my teenage daughter, Jamie, to the emergency room. For nine long hours, I stood beside my daughter wondering what caused the severe pains in her stomach. The emergency room doctor poked, prodded, and tested her as she continued to double over in pain, often retching into a plastic pan.

I had hoped the bustling activities of the Thanksgiving holiday at my oldest son's house would keep me busy—too busy to remember. But now, with my daughter recovering from surgery, we would be unable to make the trip to my son's. And the memories would linger at the edge of my mind.

One by one, the doctor ruled out ulcers, kidney problems, a stomach virus, and a pelvic infection. About midday, I felt relieved to see our family doctor. He gingerly kneaded her abdomen, causing her to shrink from his hand. I noticed he kept coming back to her right side, watching her reaction. Finally, he stepped back and told me he thought it was her appendix.

By 9:00 p.m., Jamie had her inflamed appendix removed. While her problem had disappeared on the operating table, mine had just begun.

I had hoped the bustling activities of the Thanksgiving holiday at my oldest son's house would keep me busy—so busy I wouldn't remember that Thanksgiving was the time of year my former husband, my boys' father, had chosen to commit suicide. But now, with my daughter recovering from surgery, Jamie would be unable to make the trip to my son's. And the memories would linger at the edge of my mind.

To my surprise, the simple piece of white paper in the flowerpot had my name on it. "His strength is perfect when our strength is gone," the card read. As I turned it over, I realized it was from my neighbor, Donna.

I stood at the kitchen sink, my head pounding. A lone tear trailed my face. I dialed my next-door neighbor, Donna. "Do you have any aspirin?" I asked, trying to keep my voice from quivering.

"No, but I can sure pick up some for you," she said cheerily, indicating she had to go out anyway.

I sighed. "That's all right. I really need to get out." My voice cracked a bit and I added, "This is just not a good day for me." I hung up the phone. Nothing had gone right. Thanksgiving? What a joke. I was incapable of being thankful for anything.

I drove alone to the store, my nose still red from crying. I felt so exhausted, so tired. I wondered how I would ever make this small Thanksgiving come together for my husband and two teenage kids.

I could feel myself becoming wrapped up in self-pity, my energy level plummeting. By the time I drove back to my house, I felt so weak I just wanted to crawl in bed.

Pulling into the carport, I noticed a little pot of gaily wrapped lavender flowers beside my back door. *Jamie is so loved*, I thought. My daughter's friends had shown up all week with flowers, teddy bears, and videos. I brought the flowers inside and set them on the table.

To my surprise, the simple piece of white paper in the flowerpot had my name on it. "His strength is perfect when our strength is gone," the card read. As I turned it over, I realized it was from my neighbor, Donna, even though she was busy with a large family gathering. The heaviness in my heart began to lift. Of course, I thought, she was right.

I touched the soft lavender petals, considering how thoughtless I'd been. Right there, I whispered, "Thank You, Lord, for a neighbor like Donna who cares enough to give me flowers to heal my heart."

I'm grateful that when I can't get out from under the weight of my troubles, when I can't see around my self-pity, God in His infinite wisdom provides a neighborly act of kindness to get me back on the right path.

When I returned to my pot of eggs, my husband stood by my side, shelling them with me. The smell of the roasting turkey filled the room. He wrapped one arm around me and kissed my cheek. And my heart overflowed with gratitude. ⬢

HE COMFORTS US EVERY TIME WE HAVE TROUBLE,
SO WHEN OTHERS HAVE TROUBLE, WE CAN COMFORT
THEM WITH THE SAME COMFORT GOD GIVES US.

2 CORINTHIANS 1:4

On Friendship

FROM THE PROPHET BY KAHLIL GIBRAN

And a youth said: Speak to us of Friendship.
And he answered, saying:
Your friend is your needs answered.
He is your field which you sow with love and reap with thanksgiving.
And he is your board and your fireside.
For you come to him with your hunger, and you seek him for peace.

When your friend speaks his mind you fear not the "nay" in your own mind, nor do you withhold the "ay."
And when he is silent your heart ceases not to listen to his heart;
For without words, in friendship, all thoughts, all desires, all expectations are born and shared, with joy that is unacclaimed.
When you part from your friend, you grieve not;
For that which you love most in him may be clearer in his absence, as the mountain to the climber is clearer from the plain.
And let there be no purpose in friendship save the deepening of the spirit.
For love that seeks aught but the disclosure of its own mystery is not love but a net cast forth: and only the unprofitable is caught.

And let your best be for your friend.
If he must know the ebb of your tide, let him know its flood also.
For what is your friend that you should seek him with hours to kill?
Seek him always with hours to live.
For it is his to fill your need, but not your emptiness.
And in the sweetness of friendship let there be laughter, and sharing of pleasures.
For in the dew of little things the heart finds its morning and is refreshed.

Oh, the comfort,
the inexpressible comfort
of feeling safe with a person,
having neither to weigh thoughts
nor measure words, but
pouring them all out, just
as they are, chaff and grain together,
certain that a faithful hand
will take and sift them,
keep what is worth keeping,
and with a breath of kindness
blow the rest away.

GEORGE ELIOT

*Act as if what you do
makes a difference.
It does.*

WILLIAM JAMES

A Neighbor's Warm Heart on a Snowy Night

ANNETTEE BUDZBAN

The snow had finally stopped falling. My husband worked hard as he shoveled and pushed it to form frosty mountains along our large driveway, clearing a path before leaving for his evening shift at the shop.

Later that night, the snow started falling again—fast and furious. Soon the bright white snowflakes replaced my husband's earlier efforts to make a path for our car. I stared glumly out the window. My health precluded me from getting out and shoveling the driveway for my husband's return home late that night. There was nothing I could do.

I had curled up in a chair to read when I heard the sound of a snow blower, and I wondered where it was coming from. It sounded awfully close. I figured it was just our next-door neighbor clearing the newborn snow from his driveway.

As I kept listening, though, the noise seemed to be getting closer and closer. As I glanced toward the window, I thought I saw a shadow outside. I leaned close to the cold glass and saw my neighbor's beaming face as he blew the snow from our back patio into the dark, cold winter air.

I smiled and waved back in enthusiastic thanks as I hurried to the side kitchen window for a full view of our front yard. Before my eyes lay a crisp, neatly cleared driveway.

I'd never seen a more beautiful driveway. My heart was warmed, resilient against the cold, as I surveyed the crisp snow and remembered my neighbor's smile, a smile that brightened my previously cold and dreary evening. ⬡

Little Becomes Much

CHRISTY PHILLIPPE

When Cheryl couldn't sell her home after moving to a new city, she decided to rent it out. Unfortunately, her tenants trashed the place and then skipped out before fulfilling their lease. She tried to sell the house again, but it sat on the market as she made monthly mortgage payments she couldn't afford. When foreclosure began to loom, Cheryl's friends stepped in to help.

They collected enough money to cover her next mortgage payment, buying her more time to sell the house at market value.

They found a realtor willing to help Cheryl perform necessary repairs to make her home more sellable.

And another friend—an attorney Cheryl could never afford—decided to take her case pro bono to ensure that Cheryl could stave off filing for bankruptcy.

Cheryl had been striking out, but when she shared her needs, her friends stepped up to the plate! ⬡

Tea and Sympathy

What's giving you trouble today? Your hair? Your job? Your health? Don't go it alone. If finances and time will allow you to, plan a spa and beauty day with some girlfriends—hair, nails, facials, and general pampering—or just get a few friends together for dessert and coffee at a café. Let each other know what's hardest and what's best about your lives right now. Ask for and offer prayers. And after a day of treating yourselves, you might make plans to meet again next month—only this time serving others by cooking breakfast at a homeless shelter or doing some yard work.

As the day winds down, say a prayer of thanks to God for sending you great friends. ⬢

They Said It

Refusing to ask for help when you need
it is refusing someone the chance to be helpful.

RIC OCASEK

My therapist told me the way to achieve true inner peace
is to finish what I start. So far today, I have finished two bags
of M&Ms and a chocolate cake. I feel better already.

DAVE BARRY

Things are never quite as scary when you've got a best friend.

BILL WATTERSON, CALVIN AND HOBBES

A friend is someone who helps you up when you're down,
and if they can't, they lay down beside you and listen.

ANONYMOUS

God has not called us to see through each other,
but to see each other through.

AUTHOR UNKNOWN

Remember, we all stumble, every one of us.
That's why it's a comfort to go hand in hand.

EMILY KIMBROUGH

A Day at the Salon

Hair styling by the numbers:

- According to the Bureau of Labor Statistics, there are about 750,000 barbers and cosmetologists in the United States.

- Most stylists go to school full time for 10 to 24 months.

- Americans spend $40 billion a year on hair services and beauty products.

- Stylists earn an average $18.50 an hour nationally.

- In 2001, Marco Aldany of Spain set a world record when he created 25 updos in one minute. A slightly more realistic number for many stylists is around 15 clients a day.

All figures aside, your hair salon is probably your fountain of beauty, offering cuts, color, advice, and encouragement to help you look and feel your best. It's a social hub: Just go to a small-town salon the day of a homecoming dance or prom, and you'll see the chairs packed with laughing girls having their hair swirled into French twists with tendrils. Or visit any Southern beauty shop and be prepared to answer questions about your love life if you're single, or your kids if you're married.

The salon is where women gather together to pursue beauty, something all of us pursue to some degree or another. It's become a social institution. As someone once said, "In a beauty shop, women are usually busy letting their hair down while the hairdresser is busy putting it up." ⬡

Rich is the person who has a praying friend.

JANICE HUGHES

Grandmommy Henny

POLLY HEMBREE

When our personal resources are dry, we need a little help, and one of the most wonderful ways to get that help is through the prayers of people who love us. There's something almost magically comforting about hearing yourself being prayed for, to hear someone speak your name in their prayers, and to feel the deep peace of knowing that God hears the prayers we offer for each other.

We all need good spiritual leaders, people who point us toward God's love. The Apostle Paul advised his young protégé to hold tight to his faith heritage— Timothy's grandmother and mother laid the foundation for his sincere faith in God, exemplifying God's great gift of love, power, and self-discipline. In the same way,

> Without any commotion or fuss or ceremony, her love for God just spilled out and encircled my heart. I slipped off to dreams but held God's love in my heart forever. That night has never quite left me.

memories of my Grandmother Henderson—or Grandmommy Henny, as I called her—rekindle my faith in and love for God.

I remember Grandmommy Henny's soft features, the broad smile that radiated love. Upon my arrival at her front door, she always welcomed me with a shower of kisses and generous hugs. I'm not sure she ever realized that her grand displays of affection had me spinning like I had just won a beauty pageant. Her love was genuine, and the sheer memory of it soothes my soul.

As I've grown up, I've often wondered how one little woman could be so filled with love that it would come pouring out on me unawares. Her love was supernatural, infused by God himself. For me, it was life changing.

One memory that continues to glow in my mind occurred one evening when I spent the night at her house. Before going to bed, I had gone for a glass of water. When I returned, she had already dressed for bed in her long, white gown and was kneeling on the hard floor, her body resting against the bed. Her head was lying on the covers, and her long, graying dark hair fell freely in waves down her slightly stooped back. Kneeling there with her wide white sleeves stretched out in front of her, she looked like an angel bowing to God.

Quietly climbing up on my side of the bed, I listened as she prayed aloud, thanking God for His care and kindness. The tomatoes were plentiful. The corn would be coming in soon. There would be plenty of vegetables to can for the winter. Reverend Bratton's sermon today had brought her encouragement. She felt a renewed hope that God would answer her prayers for her family members who had not completely surrendered their hearts to the Lord.

Then after a long silent time on her knees, she began with great fervency to call out the names of my grandpa, my daddy, my mamma, my uncles, my aunts, and my cousins. From there, she petitioned God for her pastor, her church, her neighbors, those in war, and random people I had never known. Each person seemed to have a special need that she addressed to God.

Her talk with God must have lasted an hour or more. And then, just as I was beginning to drift off to sleep, she began praying for me. She wanted me to know God's love. She wanted me to be strong and whole and faithful and loving. She wanted me to be filled with peace.

After closing her prayer in Jesus' name, she climbed under the warm covers with me. Without any commotion or fuss or ceremony, her love for God just spilled out and encircled my heart. I slipped off to dreams but held God's love in my heart forever. That night has never quite left me.

Memories of time spent with Grandmommy now rekindle the gift of God within me. I want to always share my faith and God's love with my children and their children—just like Timothy's grandmother and mother and my Grandmommy Henny. ⬡

WHEN A BELIEVING PERSON PRAYS,
GREAT THINGS HAPPEN.

JAMES 5:16

Son of Encouragement

ACTS 11:19-36

The Bible is filled with heroes of the faith—Abraham, Moses, David, Peter, Paul, James, and many others who performed mighty deeds. But let's not forget about some of the Bible's unsung heroes.

Jonathan, the son of Saul, was a true friend to David, even saving his life from the madness of his father. Josiah, the boy king you may not have heard of, restored God's Word to the nation of Israel and led his generation to be faithful to the Lord. Rahab, a woman of Jericho, sheltered the Israelite spies by hiding them in her roof. Timothy, Paul's young protégé, served and led churches throughout Asia Minor.

What makes someone an unsung hero? A servant's heart. One of the greatest examples of servanthood is Barnabas, Paul's sometimes partner on his missionary journeys.

Over and over again, Barnabas showed that he would do anything to help.

- He was sacrificially generous to the apostles, giving up the proceeds from selling a portion of his land (Acts 4:36).

- He protected the newly-converted Paul and helped him gain acceptance with the other believers, even going with him to meet with church leaders (Acts 9:27).

- He encouraged and taught and helped others throughout the church, serving as a kind of assistant to Paul and lavishly loving church members (Acts 11:24-26).

We all need a Barnabas every now and then—someone we know we can count on to do everything they can to help us, even if it's just offering a listening ear. And all of us need to be a Barnabas to someone else.

WHOEVER GIVES TO OTHERS
WILL GET RICHER; THOSE WHO HELP
OTHERS WILL THEMSELVES BE HELPED.
PROVERBS 11:25

God's Promises for Daily Needs

God will...

Bless you for trusting Him
*The thing you should want most is God's kingdom
and doing what God wants. Then all these
other things you need will be given to you.*

MATTHEW 6:33

Hear your prayers as you pray for each other
*Confess your sins to each other and pray
for each other so God can heal you.
When a believing person prays, great things happen.*

JAMES 5:16

Encourage you through others
Your faith will help me, and my faith will help you.

ROMANS 1:12

Come to you when you seek Him
You will search for me. And when you search
for me with all your heart, you will find me!
JEREMIAH 29:13

Help and save you
He took me to a safe place.
Because he delights in me, he saved me.
PSALM 18:19

Enable you to overcome
Yet in all these things we are more than
conquerors through Him who loved us.
ROMANS 8:37 NKJV

Fulfill His plans for you
People can make all kinds of plans, but
only the Lord's plan will happen.
PROVERBS 19:21

A Prayer of Thanks and Faith

Dear Heavenly Father,

Thank You for helping me when things are out of control. Thank You for helping me meet challenges. Thank You for sending others to comfort me. Thank You for soothing me and calming my spirit.

Today, I choose to put my confidence in You and all that You're able to do through me.

OH YEAH, LOOKING GOOD!

*It's amazing, the fearlessness we suddenly
have when we're having a good hair day.*

ANONYMOUS

If you only knew how long and hard I've worked and prayed for this, you'd know why I'm so happy and excited. I'm not bragging—okay, maybe I am just a little—but I finally bought my first house.

No matter what you've been striving toward, it feels good to experience success. In the story "Silver Smile," we're reminded that patience will be rewarded, and "Serendipity" reminds us that God has all kinds of tricks up His sleeve.

GOD WANTS ALL PEOPLE TO EAT AND DRINK AND BE
HAPPY IN THEIR WORK, WHICH ARE GIFTS FROM GOD.

ECCLESIASTES 3:13

*The feeling remains
that God is on
the journey, too.*

TERESA OF AVILA

Serendipity

MARLENE DEPLER

Let's do something here in Portland before we head out to the coast. Is there anything you want to do?" my husband asked that morning in the hotel room.

I thought we had seen most of the Portland attractions on past visits. Still, intrigued, I made a trip to the rack full of tourist brochures in the lobby. I found one advertising the Japanese Garden in Washington Park. I thought I knew vaguely where it was—it would be right on our way. So I suggested it to my husband, and he agreed.

We crossed the river to the west side of Portland and found the exit we needed. When we passed the zoo and followed the signs leading to the Japanese Garden, we also noticed signs leading in the same direction that said, "Rose Garden." We

> The air was perfumed with the sweet, delicate fragrance of roses. And then we caught our first glimpse of the hillside filled with thousands of rose bushes, color bursting in front of us.

wound through the wooded hillside and came to a large, terraced clearing that overlooked Portland. The rose garden was right next to the walkway that led up to the Japanese Garden.

We parked and started toward the rose garden first. The air was perfumed with the sweet, delicate fragrance of roses. And then we caught our first glimpse of the hillside filled with thousands of rose bushes, color bursting in front of us.

Glorious. Roses of every hue: yellow, peach, coral, pink, white, lavender, and everything in between. Roses of every type: tree roses, climbing roses, miniature roses, shrub roses, hybrid tea roses, old-fashioned roses.

We spent a long time meandering through the roses, drinking in the beauty. What a visual feast! We still took time to see the Japanese Garden, which was breathtakingly lovely as well, but for a rose gardener like me, those roses were the highlight.

As we drove away, my husband commented on the serendipity of our day—finding something so wonderful while looking for something else. In our journey through life, we occasionally have these moments. Sometimes we are aware of them, and other times we are too distracted to notice.

When have you actively pursued one goal or dream, only to stumble on a joy you weren't even looking for? Have you ever headed one direction through life and gotten frustrated by a detour, realizing later that the detour was a gift? In the midst of great sorrow or pain, have you had an unexpected encounter with grace? On an ordinary day with its mundane routine, have you ever been surprised by an unexpected blessing?

My desire is to have the eyes to see all the serendipitous blessings that come my way—and then sing thanks to God. ⬡

HE SATISFIES ME WITH GOOD THINGS AND
MAKES ME YOUNG AGAIN, LIKE THE EAGLE.

PSALM 103:5

I implore you in God's name, not to think of Him as hard to please, but rather as generous beyond all that you can ask or think.

ABBÉ DE TOURVILLE

The Smell of New Clothes

CHRISTY PHILLIPPE

A missionary and his family visited Sheila's home in the United States while raising funds. He had been serving in a warm climate and it was obvious that in the cold region where he and his family were headed next, their clothing would be inadequate. After the visit, Sheila decided to outfit the entire family with new clothes. She went shopping and sent the care package right away.

It didn't take long for a letter to come from the missionary, now a close family friend: "We cannot believe the gift you sent. All of us had forgotten how wonderful the smell of new clothes is! God bless you, our dear friends!"

Sheila knew what he was talking about, for she, too, was inhaling a lovely aroma—the sweet, wholesome fragrance of being a "dear friend." ⬡

Share the Love

On great hair days, sometimes it's easier to spread love and joy to others—and sometimes it's harder. If you're having a great day, don't forget to pass it along by boosting someone else's morale. If your sister or a coworker has been looking a little droopy, pick up a lip gloss, some eyeliner, and shadow in her colors and deliver in a cheerful makeup bag. If you have a grandparent in a nursing home, send flowers or drop by with a deck of cards and an interruption-free hour. Encouraging someone else will only make your good day better. ⬢

They Said It

Taking joy in living is a woman's best cosmetic.

ROSALIND RUSSELL

Beauty is how you feel inside, and it reflects in your eyes.
It is not something physical.

SOPHIA LOREN

If we could only see the heart of the Father, we would be
drawn into praise and thanksgiving more often. Our God is
not made of stone. His heart is the most sensitive and tender
of all. No act goes unnoticed, no matter how insignificant
or small. A cup of cold water is enough to put tears in the eyes
of God. God celebrates our feeble expressions of gratitude.

RICHARD J. FOSTER

The foolish man seeks happiness in the distance;
the wise grows it under his feet.

JAMES OPPENHEIM

If you don't think every day is a good day, just try missing one.

CAVETT ROBERT

Beauty Tips

Here are seven sure-fire beautifiers—they may not be conventional fashion-mag fare, but they come 100% guaranteed.

- Laughter: Ask a child share with you his or her favorite joke. The telling can be as fun as the punch line.

- Kindness: Do something good for someone who can't pay you back. Leave an extra $5 to help pay for the meal of the person in line behind you at the drive through—and savor the expression of surprise on his or her face.

- Servanthood: Fix a favorite, labor-intensive double-portioned dinner for your family—and take the other half over to your next-door neighbor.

- Perspective: Make a scrapbook for each of your kids, celebrating their activities, accomplishments, and all the things that make them special.

- Patience: Look for something good in someone you're in conflict with. For optimum results, tell them what you found.

- Love for life: Throw a party "just because." Make a cake and decorate and maybe even give some small favors to everyone you invite.

- Self-Confidence: Make a list of the things you like about yourself, and keep it where you'll see it often. ⬡

She Walks in Beauty

LORD BYRON

She walks in beauty, like the night
Of cloudless climes and starry skies;
And all that's best of dark and bright
Meet in her aspect and her eyes:
Thus mellowed to that tender light
Which heaven to gaudy day denies.

One shade the more, one ray the less,
Had half impaired the nameless grace
Which waves in every raven tress,
Or softly lightens o'er her face;
Where thoughts serenely sweet express
How pure, how dear their dwelling-place.

And on that cheek and o'er that brow,
So soft, so calm, yet eloquent,
The smiles that win, the tints that glow,
But tell of days in goodness spent,
A mind at peace with all below,
A heart whose love is innocent!

*Charm can fool you,
and beauty can trick you,
but a woman who respects
the Lord should be praised.*

PROVERBS 31:30

Laughter on one's lips is a sign that the person down deep has a pretty good grasp of life.

HUGH SIDEY

Silver Smile

KAREN ROBBINS

Humor is a gift from God that can see us through difficult times in life. It also sees us through ridiculous times, like the silliness of ortho-dontic appliances—braces.

"Braces? I'm a thirty-five-year-old mother of five children. I can't wear braces!" My argument was futile. In order to straighten my "fang" tooth and fill in the spaces left by two very old baby teeth that needed to be pulled, I had to look like a middle-aged teenager for a while.

"Okay, let's see Metal Mouth Mom!" my kids demanded as they burst into the house from school with wide and, as yet, un-banded grins.

"Remember," I threatened, "any and all names you create can and will be used against you when it's your turn."

"Smile" became the command of the day. Believe me, the last thing I wanted to do that first week was smile. Each time the inside of my lips slid over those little corners of metal, it felt like a thousand tiny razor blades shredding the inside of my mouth. The old dungeon masters of England couldn't have conceived a better torture.

I learned quickly that the little packet of wax I had dropped into my pocket at the orthodontist's office was my key to comfort. With a few well-placed lumps, I could smile with ease. But who wanted to see a mouthful of teeth with tumors?

Lord, help me to see the humor in this situation, I prayed fervently. *Help me to laugh even though it hurts when I do.*

As my mouth became less tender, I turned from a diet of milkshakes to the hard stuff—McDonald's hamburgers. I had been warned to cut my carrots and apples into small pieces, but no one told me I wouldn't be able to bite into something as soft as a hamburger without feeling as though my front teeth were falling out.

Desperately hungry for solid food, I tore the hamburger into little pieces with my fingers and ate it. From then on, my constant traveling companions were individually wrapped plastic knives and forks for those unplanned fast food stops.

God also blessed my husband with self-control. Each night as I donned my headgear and hopped into bed looking like Darla from *Finding Nemo*, he never burst out laughing even once. I do remember a few suspicious spasms, though.

Eating out was difficult enough, but as president of the PTA, I once had to stand in front of parents and teachers to chair a meeting after lunch. To my horror, I realized I wouldn't be able to brush first.

Our principal's wife, seeing my hand in front of my mouth and my obvious distress, volunteered to give my teeth a once-over to see if any lunch was swinging from the wires. Shortly thereafter, a toothbrush began traveling with my eating utensils.

God answered my prayers. My sense of humor sharpened. He knew I needed it to survive. When my friends moved away from me as a thunderstorm approached, I laughed and said, "At least the lightening finds me attractive."

I learned to answer "strictly FM" to those who questioned how my reception was. I even bought a T-shirt that announced that "the tin grin is in" and wore it to my next orthodontist appointment. I became a favorite patient.

A good rapport developed instantly with each teenaged metallic grin I met. We would flash our silver at each other and nod in understanding. I never did meet all those adults the orthodontist kept telling me were roaming about with teeth marching into place guided by wires, rubber bands, and headgear. Maybe they weren't smiling.

God also blessed my husband with self-control. Each night as I donned my headgear and hopped into bed looking like Darla from *Finding Nemo*, he never burst out laughing even once. I do remember a few suspicious spasms, though.

Finally, the big day arrived. Freedom! The wires, the brackets, and the bands all came off. Within minutes, it was all gone, and a beautiful white smile shone back at me in the mirror. No more fang tooth. No more gaping spaces. And no more metal. I was a free woman again.

It really hadn't been so bad after all. I almost missed the attention my silver smile had brought. And my sense of humor? Well, I could finally look at the orthodontist's framed barbed wire collection on the wall and grin.

HAPPINESS MAKES A PERSON SMILE,
BUT SADNESS CAN BREAK A PERSON'S SPIRIT.

PROVERBS 15:13

New Creature

GENESIS 32:21-32

When God inspired the words of the Bible, He did not hide the foibles and disasters of His people. We read that Moses killed a man in a fit of rage; David had an adulterous affair, then tried to cover it up by having a man killed; Solomon turned from the faith of his father and worshiped idols; Peter swore and cursed to deny he was a follower of Jesus; Paul hunted down Christians and was a feared religious persecutor. The list of "ugliness" found in Scripture goes on and on.

The good news is that when a person truly encounters God, a tremendous change happens from the inside out, and that turns even the ugliest of lives into something beautiful—

- Jacob, who stole from his brother, wrestles God and is reconciled to Esau;

- Moses turns from languishing in exile with no confidence in his own words, to boldly proclaiming freedom for slaves and leading his people into the Promised Land;

- The angry persecutor, Saul, receives a new name and becomes the greatest ambassador of love the world has ever known.

No matter how ugly your life feels today, remember that God is in the business of making all things new and beautiful. ✿

> *If anyone belongs to Christ,*
> *there is a new creation.*
> *The old things have gone;*
> *everything is made new!*
>
> **2 CORINTHIANS 5:17**

God's Promises
for Good Hair Days

God will...

Give you good things
The Lord God is like a sun and shield; the
Lord gives us kindness and honor. He does not hold
back anything good from those whose lives are innocent.

PSALM 84:11

Give you what you need to enjoy life
You give us wine that makes happy hearts
and olive oil that makes our faces shine.
You give us bread that gives us strength.

PSALM 104:15

Give you joy in salvation
You will receive your salvation with joy as
you would draw water from a well.

ISAIAH 12:3

Lighten your burdens
Accept my teachings and learn from me,
because I am gentle and humble in spirit,
and you will find rest for your lives.

MATTHEW 11:29

Be close to you in all things
I keep the Lord before me always.
Because he is close by my side, I will not be hurt.

PSALM 16:8-9

Give good and perfect gifts
Every good action and every perfect gift is from God.

JAMES 1:17

Bless you abundantly
You prepare a meal for me in front of my enemies.
You pour oil on my head; you fill my cup to overflowing.

PSALM 23:5

A Prayer of Worship and Gratitude

Dear Heavenly Father,

You are so good to me. Thank You for good days and little blessings that come so graciously, so unexpected. Thank You for meeting my needs at just the right time. Thank You for Your goodness.

Today, give me a new sense of gratitude to You for the many ways You have blessed my life.

Acknowledgements

"The Advantages of Age" © Betty Jo Mings. Used by permission. All rights reserved.

"The Classics" © Carol Genengels. Used by permission. All rights reserved.

"Don't Forget to Pray, Mommy" © Autumn J. Conley. Used by permission. All rights reserved.

"The Flight of the Thunderbird" © Patricia Cena Evans.
Used by permission. All rights reserved.

"The Fragrance of Friendship" © Christy Phillippe. Used by permission. All rights reserved.

"Garden Party" © Charlene Friesen. Used by permission. All rights reserved.

"Grandmommy Henny" © Polly Hembree. Used by permission. All rights reserved.

"Happy Thoughts" © Esther Bailey. Used by permission. All rights reserved.

"I Lost My Sanity on the Road to Phoenix" © Elaine Young McGuire.
Used by permission. All rights reserved.

"Little Becomes Much" © Christy Phillippe. Used by permission. All rights reserved.

"Miracles Often Start Small" © Stan Toler. From *God Is Never Late; He's Seldom Early; He's Always Right on Time.* Used by permission of Beacon Hill Press.

"Mowing Over the Gifts" © Mignon Murrell. Used by permission. All rights reserved.

"Mrs. Beasley Packed Her Purse" © Violet Nesdoly. Used by permission. All rights reserved.

"A Neighbor's Warm Heart on a Snowy Night" © Annettee Budzban.
Used by permission. All rights reserved.

Meet the Pick-Me-Ups team

**MARK GILROY
COMMUNICATIONS**

Mark Gilroy, founder and president of Mark Gilroy Communications, Inc., has long served the publishing industry in a variety of editorial, marketing, and management roles. Jessica Inman, managing editor, is a freelance writer and editor. You can visit Mark Gilroy Communications at www.markgilroy.com.

Thinkpen Design, LLC is a leading graphic design firm for the Christian publishing and gift market. Under the leadership of design veteran Greg Jackson, Thinkpen specializes in product design creating gift books, greeting card lines, and gifts. Visit Thinkpen on the web at www.thinkpendesign.com.

ALSO AVAILABLE FROM THE PICK-ME-UP SERIES:

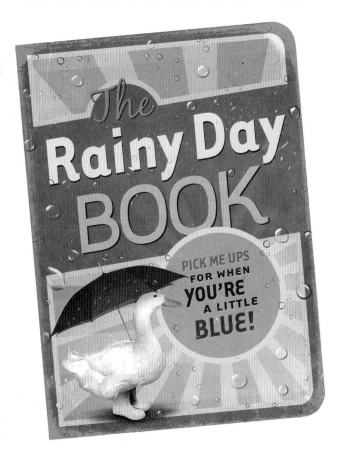

If you enjoyed *The Bad Hair Day Book*, you're sure to love *The Rainy Day Book* and *The Dog Day Book*.